Colgate University

Hamilton, New York

Written by Desireé Abeleda and Elisa Benson

Edited by Alyson Pope and Jon Skindzier

Layout by Kelly Carey

Additional contributions by Omid Gohari, Christina Koshzow, Chris Mason, Joey Rahimi, and Luke Skurman

COLLEGE PROWLER

ISBN # 1-4274-0040-7
ISSN # 1551-9732

Printed in the U.S.A.
www.collegeprowler.com

Last Updated 5/15/06

Special Thanks To: Babs Carryer, Andy Hannah, LaunchCyte, Tim O'Brien, Bob Sehlinger, Thomas Emerson, Andrew Skurman, Barbara Skurman, Bert Mann, Dave Lehman, Daniel Fayock, Chris Babyak, The Donald H. Jones Center for Entrepreneurship, Terry Slease, Jerry McGinnis, Bill Ecenberger, Idie McGinty, Kyle Russell, Jacque Zaremba, Larry Winderbaum, Roland Allen, Jon Reider, Team Evankovich, Lauren Varacalli, Abu Noaman, Mark Exler, Daniel Steinmeyer, Jared Cohon, Gabriela Oates, David Koegler, and Glen Meakem.

Bounce-Back Team: Brad Polansky, Julia Reid, and Sarah MacFarlane.

College Prowler®
5001 Baum Blvd.
Suite 750
Pittsburgh, PA 15213

Phone: 1-800-290-2682
Fax: 1-800-772-4972
E-Mail: info@collegeprowler.com
Web Site: www.collegeprowler.com

How this all started...

When I was trying to find the perfect college, I used every resource that was available to me. I went online to visit school websites; I talked with my high school guidance counselor; I read book after book; I hired a private counselor. Sure, this was all very helpful, but nothing really told me what life was like at the schools I cared about. These sources weren't giving me enough information to be totally confident in my decision.

In all my research, there were only two ways to get the information I wanted.

The first was to physically visit the campuses and see if things were really how the brochures described them, but this was quite expensive and not always feasible. The second involved a missing ingredient: the students. Actually talking to a few students at those schools gave me a taste of the information that I needed so badly. The problem was that I wanted more but didn't have access to enough people.

In the end, I weighed my options and decided on a school that felt right and had a great academic reputation, but truth be told, the choice was still very much a crapshoot. I had done as much research as any other student, but was I 100 percent positive that I had picked the school of my dreams?

Absolutely not.

My dream in creating *College Prowler* was to build a resource that people can use with confidence. My own college search experience taught me the importance of gaining true insider insight; that's why the majority of this guide is composed of quotes from actual students. After all, shouldn't you hear about a school from the people who know it best?

I hope you enjoy reading this book as much as I've enjoyed putting it together. Tell me what you think when you get a chance. I'd love to hear your college selection stories.

Luke Skurman
CEO and Co-Founder
lukeskurman@collegeprowler.com

Welcome to College Prowler®

During the writing of College Prowler's guidebooks, we felt it was critical that our content was unbiased and unaffiliated with any college or university. We think it's important that our readers get honest information and a realistic impression of the student opinions on any campus—that's why if any aspect of a particular school is terrible, we (unlike a campus brochure) intend to publish it. While we do keep an eye out for the occasional extremist—the cheerleader or the cynic—we take pride in letting the students tell it like it is. We strive to create a book that's as representative as possible of each particular campus. Our books cover both the good and the bad, and whether the survey responses point to recurring trends or a variation in opinion, these sentiments are directly and proportionally expressed through our guides.

College Prowler guidebooks are in the hands of students throughout the entire process of their creation. Because you can't make student-written guides without the students, we have students at each campus who help write, randomly survey their peers, edit, layout, and perform accuracy checks on every book that we publish. From the very beginning, student writers gather the most up-to-date stats, facts, and inside information on their colleges. They fill each section with student quotes and summarize the findings in editorial reviews. In addition, each school receives a collection of letter grades (A through F) that reflect student opinion and help to represent contentment, prominence, or satisfaction for each of our 20 specific categories. Just as in grade school, the higher the mark the more content, more prominent, or more satisfied the students are with the particular category.

Once a book is written, additional students serve as editors and check for accuracy even more extensively. Our bounce-back team—a group of randomly selected students who have no involvement with the project—are asked to read over the material in order to help ensure that the book accurately expresses every aspect of the university and its students. This same process is applied to the 200-plus schools College Prowler currently covers. Each book is the result of endless student contributions, hundreds of pages of research and writing, and countless hours of hard work. All of this has led to the creation of a student information network that stretches across the nation to every school that we cover. It's no easy accomplishment, but it's the reason that our guides are such a great resource.

When reading our books and looking at our grades, keep in mind that every college is different and that the students who make up each school are not uniform—as a result, it is important to assess schools on a case-by-case basis. Because it's impossible to summarize an entire school with a single number or description, each book provides a dialogue, not a decision, that's made up of 20 different topics and hundreds of student quotes. In the end, we hope that this guide will serve as a valuable tool in your college selection process. Enjoy!

OMID GOHARI ◯ CHRISTINA KOSHZOW ◯ CHRIS MASON ◯ JOEY RAHIMI ◯ LUKE SKURMAN ◯
The College Prowler Team

COLGATE UNIVERSITY

Table of Contents

Introduction from the Author

Forget Colgate's firm position among top-tier liberal arts universities. Disregard the sheer volume of league titles our Division I sports teams have reaped in past years. Ignore our picturesque campus, our successful alumni, and the pair of swans that live in our on-campus lake. Forget all of these things, because the image of Colgate as a university will never replace the image of Colgate as a brand of toothpaste. Why even bother trying?

All jokes aside, we believe Colgate is the perfect balance of a small liberal arts college boasting a small student-to-teacher ratio and a large university, complete with state-of-the-art resources and renowned faculty. Its traditions fortify the institution and strengthen the spirit that is Colgate. As Colgate moves closer to receiving its due recognition, placing it among great institutions such as those in the Ivy League, it remains loyal to what made it so great in the first place—its small, tight-knit community of outstanding students and faculty, and its dedication to academic excellence.

Competition for admission into Colgate increases every year. Each incoming class, according to the statistics, outshines the class preceding it. This indicates the University's growing popularity among ambitious students looking for a reputable institution comparable to an Ivy League education without the major university setting. This university is on the verge of even greater praise and acclaim.

We jumped at the chance to let the world know what an amazing institution Colgate University is. We fell in love with it, and hope that this book will give others the opportunity to do so, as well. We love Colgate University, despite all dentistry jokes. We love Colgate for the amazing experiences we have had our first two years, and hopefully in the years to come. We love Colgate for its cold winters that make us appreciate every ray of sunshine, for its late-night, moonlit walks home from downtown, and for every time we catch our breath upon arriving to campus, as if seeing the incredible brillance of campus the way we did when we moved in as freshmen.

Desireé Abeleda and Elisa Benson, Co-Authors

Colgate University

By the Numbers

General Information

Colgate University
13 Oak Drive
Hamilton, New York 13346

Control:
Private

Academic Calendar:
Semester

Religious Affiliation:
None

Founded:
1819

Web Site:
www.colgate.edu

Main Phone:
(315) 228-1000

Admissions Phone:
(315) 228-7401

Student Body

Full-Time Undergraduates:
2,796

Part-Time Undergraduates:
28

Total Male Undergraduates:
1,364

Total Female Undergraduates:
1,460

Admissions

Overall Acceptance Rate:
33%

Early Decision Acceptance Rate:
60%

Regular Acceptance Rate:
31%

Total Applicants:
6,551

Total Acceptances:
2,184

Freshman Enrollment:
737

Yield (% of admitted students who actually enroll):
34%

Early Decision Available?
Yes

Early Action Available?
No

Early Decision Deadline:
November 15

Early Decision Notification:
December 15

Regular Decision Deadline:
January 15

Regular Decision Notification:
April 1

Must-Reply-By Date:
May 1

Applicants Placed on Waiting List:
889

Applicants Accepted from Waiting List:
435

Students Enrolled from Waiting List:
44

Transfer Applications Received:
178

Transfer Applications Accepted:
45

Transfer Students Enrolled:
22

Transfer Application Acceptance Rate:
25%

Common Application Accepted?
Yes

Supplemental Forms?
Yes

Admissions Web Site:
www.colgate.edu,
click on "Admission & Aid"

SAT I or ACT Required?
Either

SAT I Range (25th–75th Percentile):
1270–1430

➜

→

SAT I Verbal Range (25th–75th Percentile):
630–710

SAT I Math Range (25th–75th Percentile):
640–720

Retention Rate:
96%

Top 10% of High School Class:
73%

ACT Composite Range:
28–32

Application Fee:
$55; waived for electronic applications

Financial Information

Full-Time Tuition:
$33,105 per year

Room and Board:
$8,065

Books and Supplies:
$870

Average Need-Based Financial Aid Package (including loans, work-study, grants, and other sources):
$23,971

Students Who Applied For Financial Aid:
48%

Students Who Received Aid:
44%

Financial Aid Forms Deadline:
January 15

Financial Aid Phone:
(315) 228-7431

Financial Aid E-Mail:
finaid@mail.colgate.edu

Financial Aid Web Site:
http://offices.colgate.edu/financialaid

Academics

The Lowdown On... Academics

Degrees Awarded:
Bachelor
Master

Most Popular Majors:
13% English language and literature
12% Economics
11% Political science and government
10% Sociology
9% History

Full-Time Faculty:
255

Faculty with Terminal Degree:
96%

Student-to-Faculty Ratio:
10:1

Average Course Load:
4 courses

➜

Graduation Rates:

Four-Year: 85%
Five-Year: 89%
Six-Year: 89%

Special Degree Options

Pre-Engineering studies; Childhood Teacher Certification and Adolescent Teacher Certification in English, history, mathematics, chemistry, biology, earth science, and physics.

AP Test Score Requirements

Possible credit for scores of 4 or 5

IB Test Score Requirements

Possible credit for scores of 5, 6, and 7

Best Places to Study

The library is the natural choice, but beware of the notoriously soporific lounge chairs, and the occasional fraternity streaking during finals week. The renovated O'Conner Campus Center—"the Coop"—also boasts an oversized fireplace, the perfect study companion for Colgate's arctic winters. Students can also reserve empty classrooms for distraction-free study sessions.

Did You Know?

? Historically, **Colgate students are required to pass a swim test**. According to campus legend, wealthy parents donated big bucks to the school after their son drowned in Colgate's Taylor Lake, but stipulated a mandatory swim test for future students. In reality, Colgate used to test students for proficiency in a variety of athletic pursuits. In 2004, the Student Government Association made the historic decision to eliminate the requirement, but agreed to let it count for PE credit.

Cooties? Colgate was all-male until 1970.

No need to add up credit hours at Colgate. **Every course counts for one credit** toward the 32 needed to graduate.

"Triskaidekaphobia" is fear of the allegedly unlucky number 13, but at Colgate, this numeral is celebrated. Campus history claims Colgate was founded by "thirteen men with thirteen dollars and thirteen prayers," which explains why Colgate is located at 13 Oak Drive, why the local "13346" zip code begins with the number 13 and ends with three digits that add up to it, and why Colgate's famous a cappella singing group is named the Colgate Thirteen.

Colgate's core curriculum, one of the oldest in the country, is the liberal arts answer to gen-ed requirements. All students take Western Traditions, Challenge of Modernity, a scientific perspective, and a non-Western culture class by the end of their sophomore year.

In summer 2004, construction began on **a $52.5 million renovation project for Colgate's main library**. The 51,000 square foot facility will debut in December 2006, complete with a robot that will retrieve books for students!

Students Speak Out On... Academics

"For the most part, you can usually find out from other students which classes and professors to avoid. I only find my classes to be boring when they turn out to be much different than I expected."

"Most of the teachers' intelligence is intimidating. Doctors abound with more than enough knowledge to push someone away using some eight plus letter word. Although these professors have their doctorates, most of them are trapped at school with you, so they are willing to spend time with a student, helping with work or simply bantering over the most mundane of subjects. Personally, **I have enjoyed all of the teachers**, and on more than one occasion, these teachers have become friends who offered me chances to do things I never hoped I could do at Colgate—funding research in Japan, or designing a lecture series come to mind.

"Classes in the afternoon interest me more than classes in the morning. As for classes being fun and interesting, **Colgate offers a wide enough variety** of such a high quality that class is always interesting."

"As with any college, **professors are hit or miss**. I feel like student-teacher evaluations are kind of useless because they are supposed to ensure that effective, well-liked professors receive tenure—but generally, it seems that the best professors are the ones that are turned away."

"The quality of teaching at Colgate is excellent. Colgate pays a great deal of **attention to student feedback** regarding the quality of the classroom experience when extending professorships—there are no publishing jockeys with poor classroom presence here. Of course, there is inevitably a certain amount of hit or miss, but Colgate keeps that to a remarkable minimum. The classes are varied and interesting—the required Liberal Arts core curriculum, in particular, has a broad range of interesting, provocative classes."

"I have run into **a few boring, arrogant professors**, but for the most part, they do a good job interacting with the students and making an effort to be readily available for extra help and explanation of material. As a psychology major, I find that I really enjoy my psychology classes, and find them fascinating (what a huge surprise!). But even the random, non-major and non-minor classes I take have something to offer and expand my knowledge."

"The classes that are interesting totally depend on which professor is teaching it. Sometimes the course material should be interesting, but the professor is dull; sometimes the course sounds boring, but the professor is amazing. My Western Traditions class, which everybody has to take (and most people hate), was **my absolute favorite class** I've taken at Colgate, because the professor was so enthusiastic and fun."

"Like other universities, I imagine, **there are some professors you shouldn't graduate without taking**, and some professors you should try to avoid. I would suggest asking around to see who the good ones are. Knowing that, there are some amazing professors at Colgate, ones not found at any other school. I would definitely recommend cashing in on their knowledge and intellect."

The College Prowler Take On... Academics

Although achieving academic excellence at a reputable university like Colgate is challenging, the majority of Colgate professors make the experience interesting and worthwhile. Professors also take advantage of the generally small class sizes with class dinners or field trips. Because Colgate has only a handful of graduate students, undergrads have many opportunities to gain lab and research experience. Many students also receive funding to continue class projects on campus during the summer, a plus for students who do not want to spend three months flipping burgers back home. The message is clear—at Colgate, education is not confined to the four walls of a classroom.

Because the core curriculum allows students ample flexibility to dabble in a variety of disciplines, Colgate is the perfect choice for undecided students. Another perk is that as early as the first year, most class sizes are small, so students often recieve a professor's full attention. Unfortunately, limited class size means courses fill up quickly, so registering for classes can be extermely frustrating; it can be difficult to get your first choice of class or professor within popular disciplines. Some advice is to be persistent—profs can, and usually will, sign you into a course with a demonstrated desire to get in it. In summary, Colgate's top-notch curriculum and accessible professors will expand and challenge your mind, but course registration is a nightmare.

The College Prowler® Grade on
Academics: A-

A high Academics grade generally indicates that professors are knowledgeable, accessible, and genuinely interested in their students' welfare. Other determining factors include class size, how well professors communicate, and whether or not classes are engaging.

Local Atmosphere

The Lowdown On... Local Atmosphere

Region:
Northeast

City, State:
Hamilton, NY

Setting:
Rural

Distance from NYC:
4.5 Hours

Points of Interest:
The Baseball Hall of Fame
Colgate is near the Finger Lakes Region in Onondaga County in Central New York
Erie Canal Sites
Harriet Tubman's house in nearby Auburn

→

Closest Shopping Malls:

Riverside Mall
5666 Horatio St, Utica
(315) 797-7171

Carousel Center
Carousel Center Dr., Syracuse
(315) 466-7000

Great Northern Mall
4155 State Route 31, Clay
(315) 622-4449

Shoppingtown Mall
3649 Erie Blvd., Syracuse
(315) 446-9160

Closest Movie Theaters:

Hamilton Movie House
7 Lebanon Street, Hamilton
(315) 824-2724

Glenwood Movieplex (20 mi)
Rt. 46, Oneida
(315) 363-6422

Clinton Cinema (21 mi)
2 Fountain St., Clinton
(315) 853-5553

Colonial Theatre (24 mi)
35 S. Broad St., Norwich
(607) 334-2135

Sangertown Square (29 mi)
Rts. 5 & 5a, New Hartford
(315) 797-2121

City Web Site

www.hamiltonny.com

Did You Know?

Five Fun Facts about Hamilton:

- Set your alarm; **every Saturday morning, Hamilton hosts a Farmer's Market** with fresh fruits and vegetables, pottery, and crafts from local vendors. Also choose from an assortment of freshly-baked goods.
- The Oneida Indian Nation considers the land adjacent to Hamilton sacred, because it **once housed members of the Iroquois League**.
- In case you missed it, Hamilton, NY made it on *The Sporting News*'s 2001 list of **the best cities for sports**—clocking in as the 212th best!
- Prior to each feature film, **the Hamilton Movie House** projects a slideshow of local people, places, and nature.
- *Golf Digest* rated Colgate's **Seven Oaks Golf Course** among the top five college courses in the country.

Students Speak Out On...
Local Atmosphere

"It's such a small town, but such a community because of it. Colgate does a really nice job of organizing "Town and Gown" events, and letting students know about things going on in town."

"It's really **nice to be able to walk everywhere**, especially when we're going out on the weekends, even though there isn't really much to walk to."

"There is a clear division in Hamilton, between the traditionally preppy, wealthy Colgate students and the 'townies' in the Hamilton area. Possibly because a large portion of Colgate students come from an affluent background, there is an underlying sense that the residents of Hamilton may resent the presence and prevalence of Colgate students. On the other hand, many Colgate students go to great lengths to establish successful community service-related projects in the town of Hamilton. There are certainly many Hamilton residents who interact regularly with these **hard-working, generous Colgate students**, and consequently think very highly of the University."

"**The town is really quaint and friendly**, but it is sleepy, and there is nothing to do beyond partying. The school tries to say that they promote other things besides drinking, but good luck trying to find stuff to do if you don't drink. I recommend bringing a car, because it is next to impossible to leave unless you have one."

"**Downtown Hamilton, NY is relatively dull**. During the day it is your typical quiet, isolated town, while Friday and Saturday nights it is a noisy, drunken mess that would be considered wholly inappropriate outside of a college town. While there are a lot of events that try to bind the town to the college, there is also a noticeable undercurrent of distrust between the so-called 'townies' and the Colgate students."

"The closest college is Hamilton University, which is a 30-minute drive away, **about half the size of Colgate**, and has even fewer social options. Your best bet to get away from life at Colgate is to drive to Syracuse (about an hour north). Also, many students will make the 30-minute trek to Walmart on the weekends for any necessities."

"**Colgate is not a suitcase school**. In any given weekend, roughly 96 percent of the student body is present on campus at any given time."

"One of the best attributes of the college is that its **rural location forces students to interact** and learn from one another both inside and outside the classroom. One could miss out on this great learning opportunity by attending a college in a major city. Regardless of if we were talking about academics or going out drinking together, I found that being able to socialize with the same people in and out of the classroom was the single most important factor in making Colgate a unique, memorable undergraduate experience."

"If you want a busy, sprawling metropolis, **Colgate is not the school for you**. It's quite small, and the closest Walmart is about 30 minutes away. However, I think that because Hamilton is so centered around Colgate, it makes a student feel like they are connected to the community. Hamilton really makes an effort to support Colgate students through discounts or special events."

"Most people stay around the Hamilton area. You're not going to find much else that is close by. On weekends, though, you can always check out Sangertown Mall (about 30 minutes away) or Carousel Mall (an hour away). There are some good movie theaters and other stuff within driving distance, but **I mostly stay around Hamilton**. With that said, I've never had a problem finding something to do."

"Hamilton is a very small community, and **Colgate is very distinct from the town**, although the college is really starting to do more to get students involved with 'downtown' projects."

The College Prowler Take On...
Local Atmosphere

Buried amongst the rolling, tree-lined hills of Central New York's Chenango Valley is Hamilton, New York, a small, college-oriented community that doubles in size when Colgate's 2,700 some students arrive for the school year. While Hamilton totes a limited array of shops and eateries, these businesses completely cater to the college kid. That means you can find anything you need, purchase it with your gatecard (student ID with a debit card feature accepted by local businesses), and probably receive a student discount. Colgate has a spirit of community that nurtures and enriches all aspects—intellectual and social—of student life. This is the kind of place where the pizza place and the florist deliver right to your dorm room door, where local restaurants offer donations and special prices for student events, and where September kicks off with a "Streetfest" featuring student bands, sidewalk sales, and a game of twister sprawled across the pavement on a blocked-off Lebanon Street.

Another major advantage to living in the middle of nowhere is that on any given weekend, more than 90 percent of the student body is still on campus. It does not turn into a ghost town with nothing to do. Most students really grow fond of Hamilton's small-town charm.

The College Prowler® Grade on

Local Atmosphere: C+

A high Local Atmosphere grade indicates that the area surrounding campus is safe and scenic. Other factors include nearby attractions, proximity to other schools, and the town's attitude toward students.

Safety & Security

The Lowdown On... Safety & Security

Number of Colgate Security Officers:

Three administrators, one department secretary, ten full time officers, five full time dispatchers, ten part time officers/dispatchers, and 29 auxiliary officers

Safety Services:

Emergency medical response
Emergency telephones
Medical transportation
Personal safety escort

Additional Services:

Fire safety awareness

Lost and found

Motor vehicle assistance

Parking permits

Photo-identification cards

Student room lockouts

Weapons storage

Health Services

Basic medical services, on-site pharmaceuticals, immunizations (including those needed for overseas travel), STD and/or pregnancy prevention, STD screening, counseling and psychological services.

Health Center Office Hours

Main Branch
Hours: Monday–Friday 9 a.m.–12 p.m., 1 p.m.–5 p.m.
Saturday and Sunday, 12 p.m.–4 p.m.; appointment required
(315) 228-775
http://offices.colgate.edu/healthcenter

Satellite Branch
Hours: Monday–Friday, 10:30 a.m.–3:30 p.m.; walk-ins only
(315) 228-7715

Counseling and Psychological Services
Hours: Monday–Friday, 8:30 a.m.–12 p.m., 1 p.m.–5 p.m.
(315) 228-7385
http://offices.colgate.edu/counseling

Did You Know?

?

Campus Safety **employs 30 to 40 students every year** to help with administrative tasks.

According to Campus Safety, **petty theft of CDs** topped the list of crimes in past years.

Students Speak Out On... Safety & Security

"The campus is extremely safe. I felt like I could walk around at any time and be okay. I never heard of anyone feeling unsafe."

"It's great! I always feel safe on campus, even late at night. There is usually someone else walking around, and there are **blue-light emergency stations everywhere**. I think I've heard that it was only used once, and the culprit was someone who needed directions, or something like that."

"**Campus Safety is everywhere**, which is a good thing in terms of safety, but it sometimes makes it difficult to get away with having a loud party in the dorms and whatnot."

"An 18-year-old girl can walk alone up the hill, drunk and tired, wearing an Armani dress and carrying a Gucci bag with a thousand credit cards in it, **and still not worry about getting mugged or heckled**."

"I've never locked my dorm room. I always walk alone at night. I've hitchhiked a few times in the cold weather. **Colgate is sort of like that movie, *Pleasantville***, where the fire department dedicates their time to saving cats in trees."

"Someone told me once that they were **pulled over twice in the same night** for having a burnt-out taillight. That's how little Campo has to do."

"I am pretty sure that the cops get so bored that they **wish for someone to commit a real crime**."

"Our Campus Safety touts itself as a **well-oiled, efficient, and powerful crime-prevention machine**. Maybe this is all true—the officers drive new vehicles, the ubiquitous blue rape-lights promise sanctuary, and parking is carefully monitored. However, I think the purported excellence of the campus security force is most directly related to the fact that Colgate students don't often murder, assault, or violently rape one another. The most frequent assignment of a Campus Safety officer on call, the official jargon and 10-4ing notwithstanding, is letting students into their locked dorm rooms."

"Personally, I never have felt unsafe on campus, nor have I had any problems with theft, but I know that it can be a problem. **Door codes are in effect** for most buildings, but anyone can find out the code without too much effort. A student just has to use some common sense and lock their doors."

"Campus Safety's number one job is writing parking tickets. There are little worries about crime or stealing, due to the **small community nature of the town**."

"Colgate is by far the safest campus I've ever seen. The **biggest risk on campus is probably alcohol poisoning**, but as long as you and your friends keep an eye out for each other, there usually is not a problem. Campus Safety means well, but they obviously aren't particularly popular amongst the student body."

"Campus Safety is almost a joke. Reading the police blotter in the newspaper will prove it. It's mostly full of 'the alarm went off in this dorm because popcorn was burned in the microwave.' I've never locked my door at Colgate, and **I've never had anything stolen**, or anybody I didn't know walk in."

"If you're a stoner, they hate you, but for normal people, it's no big deal. **But you should lock your door**."

The College Prowler Take On... Safety & Security

Although Colgate students offer divided responses as to where Campus Safety devotes most of its energy, be it to issuing parking tickets, tending to burnt-popcorn-induced fire alarms, or letting students into their locked dorm rooms, everyone agrees that the Colgate community feels safe. There are rarely worrisome incidents, so most students do not hesitate to walk alone late at night or leave their dorm room unattended and unlocked. Patrolling Campus Safety officers are practically omnipresent at all hours of the day, ready to handle any problems that may arise.

Despite Colgate's practically nonexistent crime rate, occasional thefts do catch students by surprise. Since security in residence halls is limited to a four-digit door code (often written in sharpie marker on a nearby surface), stay on the safe side and lock up. Campus Safety also makes regular rounds through campus buildings, so dorm room party hosts should keep their rowdy weekends quiet, or risk a write up. Of course, a "write up" usually doesn't mean anything except attending a Residential Education seminar targeted at the particular offense. Perhaps because the Campus Safety officers don't deal with any hardened criminals on a regular basis, they are typically a good-natured, helpful, and often an under-appreciated bunch—just don't park illegally, and mind the loud music!

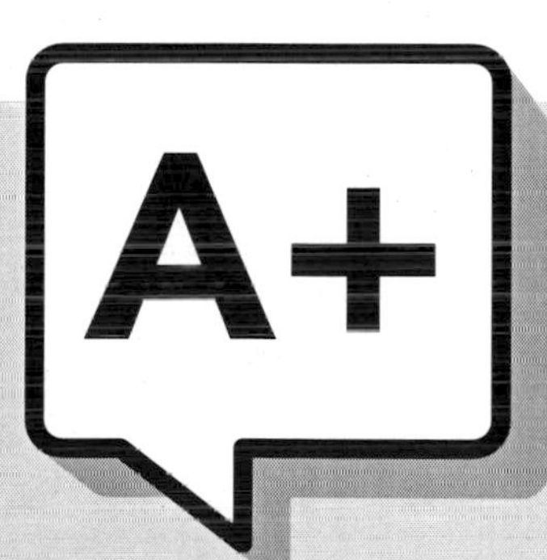

The College Prowler® Grade on

Safety & Security: A+

A high grade in Safety & Security means that students generally feel safe, campus police are visible, blue-light phones and escort services are readily available, and safety precautions are not overly necessary.

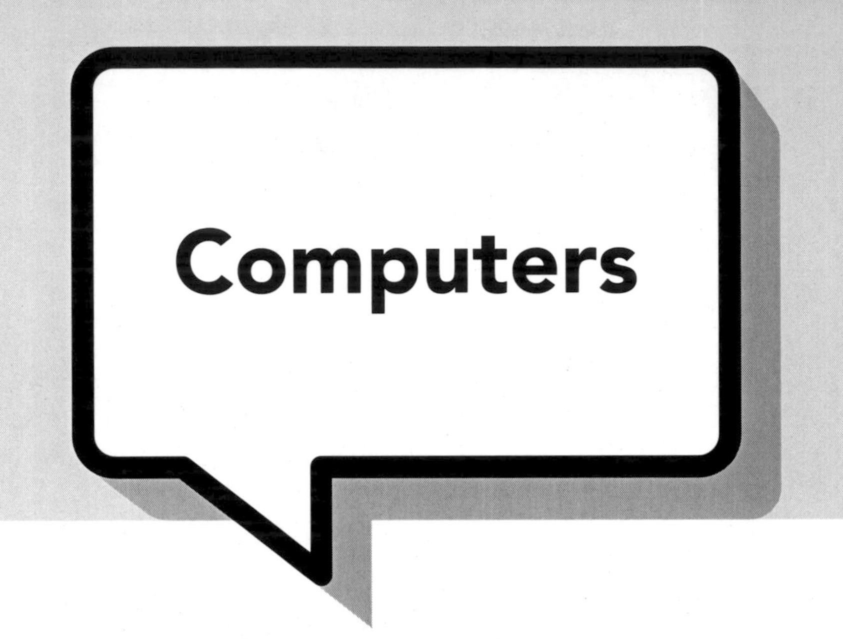

The Lowdown On... Computers

High-Speed Network?
Yes

Wireless Network?
Yes

Number of Labs:
5 main public labs; dozens more for specific departments

Operating Systems:
Mac, PC, UNIX

Number of Computers:
700 plus

Discounted Software

Academic discount available to students through the Colgate bookstore.

24-Hour Labs

Major labs stay open 24 hours during the last few weeks of classes.

Charge to Print?

No

Did You Know?

Each year, more than one hundred students work for SOURCe (Student Operated User Resource Center), the staff of trained students who tend to computer problems. When machines act up, **SOURCe can send someone directly to the residence hall to take a look**.

Students Speak Out On... Computers

"On any given day, you can usually find plenty of computers in one of the many labs on campus. However, come midterm or finals weeks, it gets difficult to get a computer in the library."

"**I've found it very helpful to have my own**. If you have a laptop, there is wireless Internet in many locations on campus, which means you can bring your computer there and have the Internet without being in a lab."

"Most Colgate students bring their own computers. **There are tons of computer labs** and portals on campus. About half of the students have laptops. While much of the campus has become wireless, the entire University will soon be wireless-ready. Over the course of the last five years, Colgate has been ranked in the top 10 schools nationwide for its computing capabilities and options for students."

"The **network is nice late at night**, or in the afternoon when it isn't clogged by users. Bandwidth is large, but easily stolen during peak hours. The school needs to find a way of getting a large trunk line and better servers, which would speed up the connections. Learn to fix your own computer, and lie to IT about bandwidth needs."

"Almost everybody has a computer, but it is not necessary, just recommended. The network has problems from time to time, but usually only briefly. **Wireless is expanding rapidly**."

"Computer labs can get pretty crowded, especially the one at the Coop and especially during the time right before, and during, midterms and finals. Also, since the **library is always being renovated**, it may be more difficult to find computer space. I would definitely advise bringing a personal computer to campus. A printer might not be necessary, though. There are a lot of places on campus to print papers and other work."

"**Definitely bring your own computer to school**. The network is often affected by viruses, and there have been a lot of problems with it this year. In general, I've noticed that Macintosh computers are not as adversely affected by these issues, so if you know how to use one, I would definitely recommend one over a PC. Also, laptops are way more convenient."

"Don't expect to find a computer in a computer lab around finals time, although there are some unknown computer labs that you can cash in on. **I would definitely bring my own computer**, and I found a laptop to be much more convenient. I'd say the easiest thing is to have your own."

"Bring your own computer no matter what. I don't care if you think you won't need it. Regardless of how many computers may be on campus, **during finals they will all be clogged** with people desperately attempting to hide the fact that they are doing nothing while attempting to write a paper."

The College Prowler Take On... Computers

More than 90 percent of Colgate students purchase a computer by their senior year, and the majority arrive with one on freshman move-in day. Although owning a personal computer eliminates the need to trudge to a public lab for every paper and research assignment, it can be more than a simple convenience when the few major labs on campus get crowded. Because the library is particularly populated during exam time, students will have to seek out the lesser-known labs on campus. There are handfuls of them buried in various academic buildings such as Lathrop, Lawrence, and Little. Students who decide to buy should opt for a laptop, to take advantage of the school's expanding wireless capabilities.

The computer network is speedy, but occasional glitches and virus outbreaks have led to one or two chunks of time sans Internet connection. Although students often point fingers at SOURCe and Information Technology Services, for the most part, these organizations keep the system up and running smoothly. It's a good thing, too, because many professors use the Blackboard system to electronically post assignments and grades. It's also a good thing for the many Colgate students who pass time by religiously checking Instant Messenger away messages, or surfing *facebook.com*, the online profile and picture service with more than 1,000 Colgate users.

The College Prowler® Grade on

Computers: B+

A high grade in Computers designates that computer labs are available, the computer network is easily accessible, and the campus' computing technology is up-to-date.

The Lowdown On... Facilities

Student Center:

The O'Connor Campus Center ("the Coop")

Athletic Center:

Reid Athletic Center

Libraries:

Everett Needham Case Library

George R. Cooley Science Library

Campus Size:

515 acres

→

Reid Center (Cotterell Court and Starr Rink):

- Basketball, gymnasium, and volleyball courts
- Bowling lanes (free of charge)
- Ice arena, utilized for men's and women's hockey as well as public free skate
- The Ledge, a computer center for student athletes

Sanford Field House:

- 6-lane 200-meter track and other track facilities
- Batting cage
- Indoor tennis courts

Huntington Gym

- Racquetball and squash courts
- Fitness center
- Basketball and volleyball gym
- Climbing wall
- Pool
- Juice bar
- Separate workout facility for varsity athletes in addition to main floor
- Sauna for relaxation and fun

Glendening Boathouse:

- Free canoe, sailboat, kayak, and paddleboat rentals
- Located on nearby Lake Morraine

What Is There to Do on Campus?

Many Colgate students are active overachievers, so they often spend free time between classes dashing off to meetings, or squeezing in a few hours at an on-campus job. In addition to normal college pursuits like eating, e-mail checking, and general socializing, the workout-crazed student body also flocks to the perpetually-packed gym. The Women's Studies Center and Environmental Studies Department each offer weekly events that combine catered lunches with lectures.

Movie Theater on Campus?

Yes; Love Auditorium—a science lecture hall by day—doubles as a free movie theater every weekend.

Bar on Campus?

Yes; Donovan's Pub in the Student Union serves alcohol, Mexican food, and a variety of other fried food delicacies.

Bowling on Campus?

Yes; there is free bowling in the Reid Center.

Coffeehouse on Campus?

No; but the Barge Canal Coffee Co. (better known as "the Barge") is a popular local coffehouse. The University sponsors a variety of free events throughout the year there, such as music performances, poetry and fiction readings, and open mic nights.

Popular Places to Chill

The recently renovated O'Connor Campus Center is a popular place for students to meet, grab a bite to eat, or just relax.

Students Speak Out On...
Facilities

"Our facilities are the best. They bought all new computers in the past few years, and completely renovated both the Coop (student center) and the fitness center. It's been fantastic!"

"I would describe Colgate as very decked out—except for Gatehouse (a freshman dorm). Everything is **very well maintained and state-of-the-art**."

"Athletics must be nice, because that is where most students seem to spend their time. Facilities are usually extremely clean as well, thank you maintenance. Sadly, not all of the facilities live up to the Colgate reputation. **The theater is hopelessly outdated**, some of the dorms range from Prince-of-Brunei big, to living in a closet with a shared bathroom, and the library is pretty limited considering we, as a school, don't have any other libraries around. One good side—everything is pretty except for the occasional dorm or theater. The student center is new and has a nice atmosphere. Too bad the money spent on its amazing and beautiful, yet utterly useless, fireplace was not put elsewhere."

"For such a small school, Colgate has good athletic facilities. **They're everything you need**, but pretty much without the 'frills' of the super-gyms at huge state schools. The computer labs are also adequate, but often, there are many network bugs, so I would recommend bringing your own machine. The student center was recently renovated—it's spectacular now!"

"For a small Division I school, the athletic facilities are pretty nice. **The fields could use some improvement**, but the athletic center is in great condition, and the field house is convenient and well kept."

"**All the student centers** have been recently revamped, or will be soon. The student center has been dubbed a 'ski lodge,' and athletic facilities have been recently replaced, too."

The College Prowler Take On...
Facilities

Colgate recently remodeled the Coop, which serves as the student center. Since receiving new furniture, floor tiles, bathrooms—new everything—it is one of the most stylish and high-traffic places on campus. Colgate spared no expense in giving students a functional and attractive place to eat, socialize, and meet for group study dates—although, the mammoth fireplace, which reportedly cost hundreds of thousands of dollars, has been a controversial addition. There is only one public gym on campus (varsity athletes have their own), and it is slightly cramped for the heavy amount of traffic it receives at peak hours. Fortunately, the school regularly adds new equipment to handle the masses.

In addition to modern and aesthetically-pleasing facilities, Colgate's beautiful campus is one of its biggest selling points. The campus boasts attractive limestone buildings stretched across a hilly, tree-lined campus. Because it is a small school, all the facilities are within a ten-minute walk. On warm September days, when myriads of students throw Frisbees on the Quad, blast music from their dorm rooms, and study in the sun. Visitors will love Colgate just as much as the students lucky enough to live there.

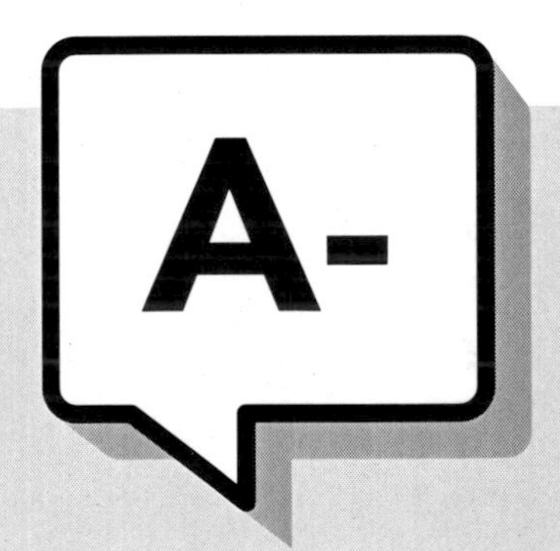

The College Prowler® Grade on

Facilities: A-

A high Facilities grade indicates that the campus is aesthetically pleasing and well-maintained; facilities are state-of-the-art, and libraries are exceptional. Other determining factors include the quality of both athletic and student centers and an abundance of things to do on campus.

Campus Dining

The Lowdown On... Campus Dining

Freshman Meal Plan Requirement?

Yes; 19 meals a week

Meal Plan Average Cost:

$3,000

Places to Grab a Bite with Your Meal Plan:

The Coop

Food: Made-to-order pasta, pizza, sandwiches, stir-fry, grill items

Location: O'Connor Campus Center

Favorite Dish: Popcorn chicken and design-your-own stir-fry

Hours: Monday–Friday 8 a.m.–10:30 a.m., 11 a.m.–2:30 a.m., Saturday and Sunday 11 a.m.–2:30 a.m.

→

→

Donovan's Pub

Location: James Colby Colgate Student Union

Food: Burgers, fries, sandwiches

Favorite Dish: Onion rings

Hours: Daily, 4:30 p.m.–8:30 p.m.

The Edge

Location: Bryan Complex

Food: All-you-can-eat, hamburgers, salad bar, vegetarian entrées

Favorite Dish: Make your own belgian waffles

Hours: Monday–Friday 9 a.m.–10:30 a.m., 11:45 a.m.–1:15 p.m., Sunday–Thursday 5:30 p.m.–7:30 p.m., Saturday–Sunday 9 a.m.–12 p.m.

Frank Dining Hall

Food: All-you-can-eat pizza, grill, hot entrée line, salad bar, dessert bar, fresh fruit, soup

Favorite Dish: Fajita night or chicken caesar salad

Hours: Monday–Friday 7:30 a.m.–9 p.m., Saturday and Sunday 11:30 a.m.–9 p.m.

Juice Bar

Location: Huntington Gym

Food: Healthy, smoothies

Favorite Dish: Herb wrapped sandwiches

Hours: Monday–Friday 11 a.m.–7 p.m.

Off-Campus Places to Use Your Meal Plan:

None

24-Hour On-Campus Eating?

No

Student Favorites:

Frank is a social mecca for first-year students. Everyone else loves the Coop.

Did You Know?

Every Sunday, Frank Dining Hall offers "Sundae Sunday," **a do-it-yourself ice cream bar** with all the fixin's. This is a major contributor to the infamous Freshman 15!

For special occasions like **Halloween and Valentine's Day**, Frank spends hours decorating the dining hall and preparing a special menu. All the employees dress in costume!

Got a birthday coming up? The best cakes around are available, surprisingly, from Frank Dining Hall. Order one by calling (315) 228-7915. (Hint: This is the perfect way for parents to send birthday wishes from afar!)

Food Vendor Day: In mid-April every year, a slew of food vendors invade Frank at lunchtime. Students can choose from dozens of different food companies to sample, and it's free even without a meal plan.

Free food abounds during finals week. Various student groups sponsor ice cream socials, pizza and wings, and other treats at the Coop.

Students Speak Out On... Campus Dining

"Dining halls here definitely leave something to be desired. The food at the Coop is good; however, it is á la carte, so it can be a lot less food for your money than the pay-to-enter dining halls."

"Honestly, **I probably only have a handful of disappointing meals each semester**. The dining halls, in addition to having pretty decent food most of the time (especially when compared to the horror stories my friends at other schools have told me!), are always open to suggestions and often turn those suggestions into actual changes. If you want something, there's a good chance you'll get it within a week!"

"Food on campus, for the majority of the time, sucks. The dining halls are nice, but **it is very hard to personalize food** when cooking for so many."

"As far as college food goes, Colgate isn't really that bad. Frank, the main dining hall, has many food options for a student to choose from. **The Coop has good food**, including stir-fry, loafer sandwiches, and wraps."

"The food is okay. **Better than most campuses**, I think. There's always cereal, salad, and sandwiches as backups, in case you don't like the main option."

"Frank sucks, but **it's really not so bad after a while**. The Coop's food is okay; service isn't. The Edge is hit or miss."

"When giving campus tours, I usually tell prospective students and families that campus food is good enough that **you can easily gain your Freshman 15**, if you are not careful. The dining halls are very concerned about variety and customer service. In every dining hall, there are comment cards available for students to fill out and submit to the staff. The dining staff, just like the rest of the University staff, has traditionally been very responsive to students' needs and wishes, one of the benefits of going to a small school."

"Frank (main dining hall) has the best food on campus. You get **the biggest selection for your money**. I'm not a very picky eater, but I've never had a problem finding something satisfying to eat. The Coop has gotten a lot better since the renovation (a little pricey for the amount of money you're allowed), but I think the sandwiches and selection are great. I eat lunch there everyday."

"My favorite thing about Frank is the workers! **They're so nice and very funny**."

The College Prowler Take On...
Campus Dining

The dining plan includes five eateries, with the infamous Frank Dining Hall being the biggest and most widely used. Frank offers a large variety of food and plenty of vegetarian options at every meal. The food is satisfying for the first few months, but after a while, picky eaters will find the regular rotations of food predictable and monotonous. The Coop has higher quality food than general Frank fare, but since they serve the same thing every week, there is also little variety. The Edge is the smallest of the dinning halls, and all too often serves the typical cheeseburger and fries entree. Because food choice at the Edge is limited, the menu is very hit or miss.

Sophomore students must remain on a meal plan, although they can limit their number of meals per week, and many don't mind a second year of school food. Because Frank serves as a central dining hall, lazy weekend brunches are a staple to both freshman social life and the rumor mill. Although food is occasionally lacking, the campus dining staff makes a genuine effort to respond to student wishes. Students can also check online menus before swiping their cards.

The College Prowler® Grade on

Campus Dining: B

Our grade on Campus Dining addresses the quality of both school-owned dining halls and independent on-campus restaurants as well as the price, availability, and variety of food.

Off-Campus Dining

The Lowdown On... Off-Campus Dining

Restaurant Prowler: Popular Places to Eat!

Amy's Hideaway Café

Food: Sandwiches, soup, salads

20 Utica St.

(315) 825-0107

Cool Features: Breakfast served all day.

Price: $10 and under per person

Hours: Monday–Friday 6 a.m.–2 p.m., Saturday and Sunday 7 a.m.–3 p.m.

Barge Canal Coffee Co.

Food: Soup, bagels, desserts

37 Lebanon St.

(315) 824-4331

Cool Features: Musical performances, open mic nights, poetry and fiction readings.

Price: $10 and under per person

Hours: Monday–Thursday 7 a.m.–11 p.m.,Friday and Saturday 7 a.m.–1 a.m., Sunday 7 a.m.–10 p.m.

→

Colgate Inn

Food: American

1 Payne St.

(315) 824-2300

Cool Features: The Colgate Inn contains three restaurants, one is only open during the summer.

Price: Tap Room, $15 and under per person; The Corner Grill (summer), $25 and under per person; dining room, $20 and under per person

Hours: Tap Room: Daily, 11:30 a.m.–10 p.m.

Dining Room: Thurday–Saturday 5 p.m.–9:30 p.m.

Country Inn

Food: Sandwiches, soup, salads

Route 12B

(315) 824-1150

Cool Features: The popular "Hungry Man" breakfast skillet has earned a cult following for its $4.25 price tag.

Price: $10 and under per person

Hours: Monday–Thursday 6 a.m.–8:30 p.m., Friday and Saturday 7 a.m.–9 p.m., Sunday 7 a.m.–1 p.m.

Hamilton Bakery

Food: Bakery

34 Utica St.

(315) 824-9400

Price: Under $5 per person

Hours: Daily, 6 a.m.–6 p.m.

Hamilton Inn

Food: American/seafood

East Lake Rd.

(315) 824-1245

www.thehamiltoninn.com

Cool Features: On Wednesday, certain entrees are discounted for students.

Price: $25 and under per person

Hours: Daily, 5:30 p.m.–9 p.m.

Hamilton Whole Foods

Food: Healthfood/organic

28 Broad St.

(315) 824-2930

Price: $10 and under per person

Hours: Monday–Saturday 10 a.m.–5:30 p.m.

Main Moon

Food: Chinese

8 Utica St.

(315) 824-1830

Price: $10 and under per person

Hours: Monday, Wednesday, and Thursday 11 a.m.–10 p.m., Friday and Saturday 11 a.m.–11 p.m., Sunday 12 p.m.–10 p.m.

→

New York Pizzeria (aka Slices)

Food: Pizza and wings

39 Lebanon St.

(315) 824-2112

Price: $1.25 for a slice!

Hours: Daily 4 p.m.–2:30 a.m.

Delivers to dorms

Nichols & Beal

Food: American

Corner of Lebanon & Utica Sts.

(315) 824-2222

Cool Features: Late-night drink specials

Price: $15 and under per person

Hours: Tuesday–Thursday 11 a.m.–9 p.m., Friday and Saturday 11 a.m.–10 p.m., Sunday 11 a.m.–9 p.m.

Numero Uno

Food: Italian/Greek

22 Lebanon St.

(315) 824-0489

Price: $4–$12 per person

Hours: Tuesday–Saturday 11 a.m.–10 p.m., Sunday and Monday 4 p.m.–10 p.m.

Oliveri's Pizzeria

Food: Pizza, wings

14 Lebanon St.

(315) 824-4444

Price: $6–$12 per person

Hours: Daily, 11:30 a.m.–1 a.m.

Parkside Deli/Café

Food: Deli

20 Broad St.

(315) 824-3015

www.parkside-deli.com

Price: $5–$10 per person

Hours: Monday–Thursday 8 a.m.–7:30 p.m., Friday and Saturday 8 a.m.–8:30 p.m., Sunday 9 a.m.–7:30 p.m.

Roger's Market-Deli

Food: Deli sandwiches, pasta salads, soups

41 Lebanon St.

(315) 824-3640

Price: $4–$8

Hours:Monday–Friday 7 a.m.–9 p.m., Saturday 9 a.m.–9 p.m., Sunday 11 a.m.–4 p.m.

Seven Oaks Club House

Food: American

East Lake Rd.

(315) 824-4420

Cool Features: Overlooks the golf course.

Price: $20 and under per person

Hours: Monday–Saturday 11 a.m.–9 p.m., Sunday 11 a.m.–8:30 p.m.

→

→

Sushi Blues

Food: Sushi

18 Broad St.

(315) 825-0225

Price: $10–$15 per person

Hours: Monday–Thursday 5 p.m.–9 p.m., Friday and Saturday 5 p.m.–10 p.m., Sunday 5 p.m.–8 p.m.

Best Pizza:

Slices (New York Pizzeria)

Best Breakfast:

Amy's Hideaway Café

Best Wings:

Oliveri's Pizzeria

Best Healthy:

Hamilton Whole Foods

Best Place to Take Your Parents:

Hamilton Inn

Student Favorites:

Slices

Nichols & Beal

Roger's Market-Deli

Closest Grocery Stores:

Tops Friendly Market

Rt. 12B
Hamilton

(315) 824-3088

Byrne Dairy

31 Utica St.
Hamilton

(315) 824-1107

Students Speak Out On...
Off-Campus Dining

"The local restaurants are pretty mediocre. There isn't much variety. Roger's probably offers the best value for your money at $4 a sub. The Tap Room is decent, too."

"**Pretty good dining fare is offered** at all the restaurants around town. For a small community, there are actually quite a few restaurants. Parkside Deli offers wonderfully fresh sandwiches, salads, soups, and delicious bakery items—cookies and muffins. Sushi Blues offers Japanese cuisine; Main Moon offers Chinese food."

"**The Colgate Inn** has a casual dining area and a nicer area for formal events; Nichols & Beal offers a good variety of bar and grill food, and the atmosphere is very relaxed. Oliveri's is the home of pizzas, Italian subs, and deep-fried goodness; Numero Uno offers Italian and Greek entrees—a good restaurant for a casual date or dinner with friends. The Barge Canal coffee shop offers many delicious coffee drinks, soups, and sandwiches, and pastries can be enjoyed while studying and listening to music or just hanging out with friends."

"For such a small town, **the food is excellent**, and many of the restaurants cater to the tastes of the typical college student, such as the delis (Parkside and Roger's) and the coffee house (the Barge). There are also classier restaurants, like the Hamilton Inn, for those special occasions."

"Most of the **restaurants off campus are a bit expensive**. Main Moon has good lunch specials, but you may need to work up the ability to stomach the food."

"The town is small, but despite the size there are **a bunch of good places to eat**. The Hamilton Inn is, by far, the best meal in town, and people often go for birthdays, dates, or to bring their families. The Colgate Inn, located right in the center of town, is operated by the school and offers a few different dining choices. The service can be slow (compared to the fast paced tri-state area), but the food is good and the atmosphere is pleasant. Parkside and Roger's are both great delis. Parkside has huge portions, really interesting sandwiches, and is always swarming with Colgate kids. Rogers is more moderately priced and also more low key."

"The restaurants in the town of Hamilton are not worthy of the New York City five-star label, but they are definitely an excellent choice when one is sick of Frank or Edge Café dining halls. **The choices are limited to American, Italian, Japanese, or Chinese**; however, some are better than others. Sushi Blues is a great spot, although pricey. On the less expensive side would be Numero Uno, where you can get quality Italian pasta dinners with a Greek dessert. Oliveri's Pizza, Parkside Café, and New York Pizzeria (called 'Slices' by the students who know the motto "slices come plain only" there) are great places for a late-night bite, especially on the weekends."

"Amy's Hideaway Café is a bit **hard to find, but it's a great place** for weekend breakfast. Parkside is classic, and Roger's has great sandwiches that you can eat at the coffee shop, the Barge (Roger's doesn't have seating of its own)."

"For pizza, all you need to know is Slices. Oliveri's makes awesome subs (the chicken parm is legit!). Hamilton definitely isn't lacking on the Italian restaurants. For sandwiches, hit up Parkside, **a little pricey, but well worth it**."

"I particularly like the Seven Oaks Club house restaurant. I think **the food is really good**, and it's more reasonably priced than the Colgate Inn or the Hamilton Inn."

"**I'm a big fan of Sushi Blues**. The sushi is very high quality, and they have lots of choices on the menu. They'll even deliver to your dorm. There are two good places to have your parents take you to when they visit—The Tap Room at the Colgate Inn, and Nichols and Beal."

"The off-campus restaurants are okay, but there aren't many to choose from or a great variety. If you want your basic Wendy's, good luck (it isn't anywhere nearby). The existing restaurants have a **decent atmosphere and a small-town vibe**."

"**I don't care what they say** about Main Moon, I think their food is decent, cheap, and it has never made me sick."

"I love Roger's Deli. **They have everything**, and their chicken salad sandwiches are the best!"

The College Prowler Take On...
Off-Campus Dining

For a small town, Hamilton offers a surprising array of high quality, tasty choices. Roger's Deli is a huge favorite for its order-as-you-like-it sandwiches and great prices. Parkside Deli is also popular, though more expensive, but they serve meals and salads, in addition to an inventive array of sandwiches. Main Moon, Hamilton's only Chinese restaurant, is the source of much controversy, as some people swear by its weekend buffet, others swear it causes indigestion. Nichols & Beal is the newest restaurant, catering to the general public by day, with a wide variety of creative entrees and sandwiches, and catering to upperclassmen students at night, with a trendy bar and late-night drink specials.

Of course, one cannot attend Colgate without loving Slices, the infinitely popular pizza spot that is actually named, but never called, New York Pizzeria. The term "Slices" actually shifts meaning depending on the context, as it can be used to refer to both the restaurant ("I'll meet you at Slices"), and the individual pie pieces themselves ("Let's order slices for delivery"). So does all this terminology get confusing? Not if you love Slices like Colgate kids do. Slices is a mandatory late-night weekend stop, and it's an awesome place to run into at least five people you know.

The College Prowler® Grade on

Off-Campus Dining: B-

A high Off-Campus Dining grade implies that off-campus restaurants are affordable, accessible, and worth visiting. Other factors include the variety of cuisine and the availability of alternative options (vegetarian, vegan, Kosher, etc.).

Campus Housing

The Lowdown On... Campus Housing

Room Types:

First-year: Singles, doubles, triples, quads

Sophomore year: Singles, doubles, triples, quads, 5- or 6-person suites

Junior year: 3–6 person apartments, Greek and theme housing

Senior year: 3–6 person apartments, Greek and theme housing

Best Dorms:

Andrews

Bryan

Bunche House

Worst Dorms:

92 Broad

Gate House

Undergrads Living on Campus:

80%

Number of Dorms:

9

Number of University-Owned Apartments:

4, plus the Broad Street Community Houses

Dormitories:

All dormitories contain a recreation area, study lounges, laundry facilities, and bicycle storage, and are wired for cable TV, telephone, and wireless high-speed Internet.

Andrews Hall

Floors: 4 plus basement

Total Occupancy: 126

Bathrooms: Shared by floor

Coed: By room

Residents: First-year

Room Types: three-, four-, and five-person suites

Special Features: TV/VCR, foosball table and ping-pong table in recreational lounge, kitchenette

Inside Scoop: Andrews is considered the party dorm.

Bryan Complex

(Four Wings: Cobb, Crawshaw, Parke, and Russel)

Floors: 3 plus basement

Total Occupancy: 54 in each complex

Bathrooms: Shared by suite

Coed: By suite

Residents: Some first-years, mostly upperclassmen

Room Types: Single and double occupancy within suites

(Bryan Complex, continued)

Special Features: Fireside lounges, TV/VCR, pool table, foosball, ping-pong. Crawshaw houses the Harlem Renaissance Center (HRC), a community for students interested in African/African American history and culture. Bryan Complex is also home to The Edge dining hall.

Inside Scoop: Despite a somewhat removed location, Bryan's suite-style living and in-house dining hall makes it one of the best residential options for sophomores

Curtis Hall

Floors: 5 plus basement

Total Occupancy: 288

Bathrooms: Shared by floor

Coed: By room

Residents: First-year, sophomores, juniors, seniors

Room Types: Doubles; 5 four-person suites and 1 six-person suite are reserved for upperclassmen

Special Features: Computer lab, kitchenette, elevator. Basement houses the Sexual Crisis Resource Center and the Satellite Health Clinic.

Inside Scoop: Curtis doubles are the smallest rooms on campus.

Cutten Complex
(Four Wings: Brigham, Read, Shephardson, and Whitnall)

Floors: 3 plus basement

Total Occupancy: 53 in each building

Bathrooms: Shared by suite

Coed: By suite

Residents: Upperclassmen

Room Types: Single and double occupancy within suites

Special Features: Cutten Dining Hall, Read House is a healthy living community

Inside Scoop: Cutten's proximity to athletic facilities makes it an ideal choice for athletes.

Drake Hall

Floors: 6 plus basement

Total Occupancy: 189

Bathrooms: Shared by floor

Coed: By room

Residents: Sophomores

Room Types: Doubles, triples, 9 four-person suites, 3 five-person suites (with in-room bathrooms)

Special Features: Music practice room, kitchenette, elevator

Inside Scoop: Drake's two "sky suites" are the most sought after dorm rooms on campus. Each sky suite contains a large common room, bathroom, and lofted bedrooms.

East Hall

Floors: 5 plus basement

Total Occupancy: 112

Bathrooms: Shared by floor

Coed: By room

Residents: First-year

Room Types: Singles, doubles, triples, two four-person suites

Special Features: Substance-free, Houses the Center for Women's Studies and the Center for Outreach, Volunteerism, and Education (COVE) on the first floor

Inside Scoop: Fifth floor residents have the benefit of roomy suites, but the nearest bathrooms are on the fourth floor.

Gate House

Floors: 2

Total Occupancy: 113

Bathrooms: Shared by floor

Coed: By room

Residents: First-year

Room Types: Doubles

Special Features: Air conditioning, computer lab, TV/VCR, pool, ping-pong and foosball tables in recreation lounge

Inside Scoop: Gate House is the biggest residential joke on campus. The temporary dorm allegedly arrived on the back of a truck when Colgate had an unexpected surge in admissions acceptances.

Stillman Hall

(Three Wings: East, Center, and West)

Floors: 4 plus basement

Total Occupancy: 140

Bathrooms: Shared by floor

Coed: By floor

Residents: First-year

Room Types: Singles, doubles, four-person suites

Special Features: Recreation lounge, TV/VCR, microwave, pool, ping-pong, foosball tables

Inside Scoop: All three wings of Stillman are connected through the attic and basement.

West Hall

Floors: 5

Total Occupancy: 112

Bathrooms: Shared by floor

Coed: By floor

Room Types: Singles, doubles, triples, two four-person suites

Special Features: Built-in wardrobes for closet space, multimedia classroom doubles as a study lounge by night

Inside Scoop: West is the oldest building on Colgate's campus. It was built as an engineering project for its students long ago.

Upperclassman University-Owned Apartments:

All apartment buildings are coed. Each apartment is fully furnished and contains a living room, dining room, and kitchen.

Newell Apartments

(Four buildings; eleven apartments per building)

Floors: 2 plus basement

Total Occupancy: 135 per building; 540 total

Bathrooms: 1.5 in each apartment

Room Types: 37 three-person; 6 four-person

Special Features: Laundry

Inside Scoop: With so many students in each complex, the Newell apartments are always a social hot spot.

Parker Apartments

(45 separate apartments)

Floors: 2

Total Occupancy: 200 total

Bathrooms: One in each four-person; one and a half in each six-person

Room Types: Ten six-person; 35 four-person

Special Features: Duplex apartments

Inside Scoop: The two-story Parker apartments feel more like townhouses than campus housing.

➔

Town House Community

(14 houses, 2 apartments per house, 8 people per apartment)

Total Occupancy: 224

Bathrooms: One double bathroom in each apartment

Room Types: Four doubles in each apartment

Special Features: New living room, dining room, full kitchen with two refrigerators, microwave, stove

University Court Apartments

Ten buildings; four apartments per building)

Floors: 2

Total Occupancy: 16 per building; 160 total

Bathrooms: One in each apartment

Room Types: 2 double occupancy bedrooms in each apartment

Special Features: Laundry housed in building #6

Inside Scoop: Learn the lingo—everyone refers to this complex as the Birch Apartments.

Broad Street Community

This community consists of individually themed interest houses. It is a cooperative environment where students share domestic responsibilities. Current houses include:

94 Broad Street
Asia Interest House

Bunche House

La Casa Pan-Latina Americana

Class of 1934 House

Creative Arts House

Cushman House

The Loj

Greek Houses

Beta Theta Pi

Delta Delta Delta

Delta Upsilon

Gamma Phi Beta

Phi Delta Theta

Phi Kappa Tau

Kappa Alpha Theta

Sigma Chi

Theta Chi

Housing Offered:

Singles: 5%

Doubles: 23%

Triples/Suites: 38%

Apartments: 22%

Other: 12%

Bed Type

Twin extra-long (80 inches)

Available for Rent

Microwaves, mini-fridges

Cleaning Service?

All shared bathrooms are cleaned regularly. Bathrooms within suites (as in sophomore dormitories) are cleaned weekly. University Apartment bathrooms are not cleaned.

What You Get

Bed, desk and chair, dresser, closet or wardrobe, window screens, cable TV jack, Ethernet or broadband Internet connections, free on-campus phone calls. All campus residents get free cable.

Students Speak Out On...
Campus Housing

"In the first-year dorms, go for a suite, they offer a lot of space, and up your odds for getting a roommate that you really like."

"**Andrews suites are the nicest**—they have large bay windows and mantelpieces over old fireplaces that make the common rooms really feel like a homey living room. Gate House was temporary housing that they never tore down—enough said."

"**The dorms are great**. Freshmen live on the top of the hill in the residential quad, right next to the academic quad, so getting to class is super easy if you wake up late. Andrews Hall offers the nicest rooms for freshmen—all are 3–6 person suites with a common room, making it easy to have large gatherings of friends. East Hall is very clean, because it's substance-free, meaning that no drugs or alcohol are permitted inside the dorm, and it's very quiet. Curtis is the newest freshman dorm, but it has the smallest rooms. Stillman is good for those who like to party, but bad for those who hate the smell of alcohol in the stairwells. West is a pretty good balance of social gatherings and study time."

"**One hall to avoid is the Gate House**. It was built as temporary housing in the '80s, and well, 20 years later it's still here. You're almost always guaranteed to see holes in the drywall and unidentifiable substances in the bathrooms after weekend parties."

"Housing for upperclassmen is good. **The apartments are all really nice and very spacious**."

"The dorms are really, really nice. Andrews Hall and Stillman are the best for freshmen, because they are suites. **No one wants to live in Gate House**. The rooms in Curtis aren't very big, either."

"Curtis and Stillman are key because they are really close to the main dining hall, Frank, but they're farther away from the Coop (O'Connor Campus Center), which houses the mail center, another dining site, study room (with a crazy looking, spaceship-like fireplace) and a great computer lab. Gate House is sort of peripheral; most people complain about getting stuck in that dorm. Andrew's rooms are huge compared to the doubles in Curtis, though there are some suite rooms in Curtis on the first floor which can house up to four people (and also on the fifth floor, but you can only live there as a sophomore). **Andrews and Stillman/West Stillman are the most centrally located dorms**. You can get up, get dressed, brush your teeth, grab your books, and practically long jump to your first class."

"After freshman year, your **names get placed in a housing lottery**—getting the number 1 would mean you have first choice of where you want to live the following year—getting number 452 means you better make friends with the person who got number 1. Lofting, if possible, is a good idea for your two beds in a double; it gives a lot more floor space, for say, yoga or Beirut tables."

"The dorm to go for freshman year is East Hall. I think it tends to have the best atmosphere for a new student. The main sophomore dorms each have their pros and cons. **I lived in Cutten last year**, and it was great."

"The dorms are adequate—not the best I've seen, not the worst I've seen. Definitely avoid Gate House (aka the projects of Colgate). Curtis has really small rooms. The **cleanest, quietest, and most diverse dorm** is East Hall."

"I love the dorms. I've had such a great experience in the two years I was in a dorm that I'm actually sad to be living in an on-campus apartment next year. Colgate does a great job of making sure facilities are working and clean and for the most part, new. Avoid Gate House, though. At any rate, first-years living in Gate House are proud of their living status. **It's actually a big joke on campus**."

"There's quite a bit of variety in terms of housing, especially once you become a junior. **Most rooms are pretty small**, especially the doubles at Curtis. Some of the suites in Andrews have nice big common areas (and a small area for the actual beds). I transferred, so I don't really know that much about freshman dorms. All of them are close enough to class, though, so I would not choose a dorm based on how close it appears to be to the Quad—that would be unnecessary."

"The '**sophomore slums**' (Bryan and Cutten complexes) are pretty ugly, but you don't have to share the bathroom with the entire floor, which is nice. I personally like the three-single suites (three single rooms and a shared bathroom). For upperclassmen, there are special interest houses and apartments. The best house for getting a single room is Bunche House, followed by 94 Broad (though the latter is a pretty old and ugly house). The apartments have mostly double rooms, with a few exceptions (there are some three-people apartments with one double and one single). I lived in Bunche House and the chef was really good."

The College Prowler Take On...
Campus Housing

For first-year students—who all live in neighboring dorms on "the hill," the popular spots are Andrews and Stillman, the two residential halls that offer suite-style living. Two double bedrooms share a common room, so the extra space is a key attraction. Sophomores with good lottery numbers end up in Cutten or Bryan, dorm complexes that offer perks like personal bathrooms. Unlucky sophomores get stuck in Drake or Curtis, traditional double style residence halls. The University Apartments for upperclassmen are large and community-oriented. Many students also opt to live in Greek houses or special interest residences. These special interest houses have access to a large pool of funds that can be used to plan in-house social events for the larger campus.

Students agree that freshmen should avoid Gate House, the butt of every campus housing joke. Although it's difficult to measure whether the shoddy conditions and poor location of Gate House are really as bad as students say, one former resident offers this advice—"If they put you in Gatehouse, transfer." The Townhouse Community is rather new, and hence the best housing available for upperclassmen.

The College Prowler® Grade on

Campus Housing: B

A high Campus Housing grade indicates that dorms are clean, well-maintained, and spacious. Other determining factors include variety of dorms, proximity to classes, and social atmosphere.

Off-Campus Housing

The Lowdown On... Off-Campus Housing

Undergrads in Off-Campus Housing:

20% (Only a certain number of seniors are permitted to live off campus)

Popular Areas:

DU Annex, apartments downtown above local merchants

Best Time to Look for a Place:

Begin looking for senior year housing second semester of sophomore year.

Students Speak Out On...
Off-Campus Housing

"It's certainly more to deal with than living on campus (rent, utilities). But it's worth it. My roommates and I made the decision to live off campus at the last possible second, and I'm really glad we did."

"**There really isn't off-campus housing**. Seniors are allowed to apply for off-campus housing, but there isn't much available, which doesn't matter too much, because the on-campus apartments are fully equipped."

"Off-campus housing at Colgate means the University-run apartments for juniors and seniors that are right on campus. **They are very nice**. There are a limited amount of non-University run apartments and houses in town that seniors must apply for."

"You have to enter into an off-campus lottery, because there's limited housing. **It's really competitive** to get houses and apartments off campus, but they're worth it, because they're beautiful. The only downfall is that it's a far walk from academic buildings."

"Everyone lives on campus for at least the first three years, unless you go abroad. **Off-campus housing is a hassle because you have to sign up early**."

"Off-campus housing is **only available for seniors** drawn from a lottery. Everyone else must live on campus all four years; on the upside, on-campus housing for juniors and seniors includes apartments owned by Colgate, but not attached to Colgate. That means you get free cable, Internet, and utilities in an apartment similar to off-campus living at other schools."

"I will tell you that living off campus is going to be **one hell of a hike in the snow**, considering the Cruiser (shuttle bus) is never on time."

"Students at Colgate are not allowed to live off campus until senior year, and even then **only about 35 percent of the seniors are able to**. This may sound terrible to prospective students, but all juniors and the rest of the seniors live in on-campus apartments that are really nice and quite removed from the rest of campus. So even though you wouldn't technically be able to live 'off-campus' until senior year, the apartment complexes make a really great community and a fun place to live. Parties there are always fun, especially since most of your friends live very close by."

The College Prowler Take On...
Off-Campus Housing

Students are divided on the off-campus living situation. Many agree that the hassle of seeking out an apartment, applying for it, and then actually dealing with utilities and rent may not be worth the feeling of independence and ownership. On the other hand, certain off-campus houses and apartments are in great shape, and many students feel like they would miss out if not engaged in the competition for one. Because Hamilton is such a small community, any off-campus residence would still be within about 20 walking minutes of the college.

Because the University apartments are well maintained, roomy, convenient, and segregated enough from campus that they escape Colgate's watchful eye, the novelty of living off-campus may be more important than the actual benefits. Students who decide to pursue off-campus options should begin looking as early as sophomore year. Hamilton has a limited selection of available rentals, so students need to claim their residences. After securing a spot, students can only cross their fingers and hope to be one of the lucky rising seniors permitted to live off-campus. There is no formal assistance for finding housing, and the off-campus parties students attend as underclassmen provide their primary exposure to local living options.

The College Prowler® Grade on

Off-Campus Housing: C

A high grade in Off-Campus Housing indicates that apartments are of high quality, close to campus, affordable, and easy to secure.

The Lowdown On... Diversity

Native American:
1%

Asian American:
6%

African American:
4%

Hispanic:
4%

White:
80%

International:
5%

Out-of-State:
65%

Most Popular Religions

Although the various religious groups actively advertise their events in hope of gaining new attendees, for the most part the groups are quiet, and the bulk of their activity takes place off campus. Christianity is the main religion on campus, but 20 percent of Colgate students are Jewish.

Gay Pride

Colgate is an open-minded community with a small LBGTQ population, so tension over sexual orientation is practically nonexistent. The Rainbow Alliance offers a support group for students, although it maintains a low profile on campus.

Economic Status

Colgate students carry designer handbags, flip the collars on their Polo shirts, and drive new models of SUVs. The school is noticeably upper-class, which may cause students from less fortunate backgrounds to feel uncomfortable.

Minority Clubs

The minority clubs maintain a visible role in campus affairs. They are often seen at the Coop standing next to tables, informing students of various events or issues. Groups work with one another in their philanthropic endeavors, such as the Brothers Charity Auction and Latin American Student Association (LASO) dance showcases.

The ALANA Cluture Center is the African, Latin American, Asian, and Native American center on campus. ALANA hosts several open-to-all speakers, brown bag lunches, and educational and social programs throughout the year.

Students Speak Out On...
Diversity

"As a rising senior, I've seen Colgate undergo many changes in the last few years. The increasing diversity with each new incoming class is noticeable."

"**I'm impressed with the administration's efforts** to improve campus diversity even more, and sort of wish I could stick around another few years to see what changes take place next."

"The campus **does not seem so diverse** as the brochures say."

"The campus is not diverse at all. True, I come from an extremely diverse high school, but it seems everyone from Colgate is rich and white. **I never felt at all poor until I went to Colgate**. The school is very divided, both in terms of race and socioeconomic class."

"There are so many international students, and they are so nice. **My roommate was from Venezuela, and one of my best friends was from Argentina**. There is something for everyone at this school."

"The campus is not at all diverse. Unfortunately, Colgate is one of the least diverse schools in the country. However, consistently greater efforts have been made each year to try to change this. **It's one of the few problems at Colgate**."

"I think it lacks a lot of times. **Where are the Hispanic people**?"

"**Diversity—what diversity**? I would like to see more, but you know what—the lack of diversity makes me stand out in a crowd of Caucasian students. I love white people, though."

"I came from an almost all-white high school, and it was great to be surrounded by all ethnicities and backgrounds. It is such a **wonderful cultural experience**."

"Colgate is not very diverse. **The school is trying**, and you can find people of different backgrounds if you look for them (join a cultural organization or hang out at ALANA). Most students are white and upper-middle-class, though. There's a reason why Colgate is known as a J.Crew campus."

The College Prowler Take On...
Diversity

The school is making efforts to attract a broader range of students, but presently, the school is still a largely homogenized group of wealthy, Caucasian students. Many of the minority students who do choose Colgate are often attending specifically for sports programs. Colgate has taken a proactive approach to addressing the problem, by focusing on diversity during freshman orientation and assuring students that diversity on campus will improve in years to come.

Although there is little visible tension between different ethnic or social groups, there is also little interaction. Some of the more integrated organizations on campus are the student dance groups, which often flaunt performers of several ethnicities during each end-of-semester Dancefest performance.

The College Prowler® Grade on

Diversity: D

A high grade in Diversity indicates that ethnic minorities and international students have a notable presence on campus and that students of different economic backgrounds, religious beliefs, and sexual preferences are well-represented.

The Lowdown On...
Guys & Girls

Men Undergrads:	**Women Undergrads:**
48%	52%

Birth Control Available?

Yes, at the Student Health Center.

Social Scene

Students are very involved in the Colgate scene. Over 85 percent are involved in varsity, club, IM, or RecSports. Students believe in the traditional Colgate "hello," and smile to others as they walk past, but not everyone does so. Some greet only those they know or who are like them, others greet everyone. In addition to the many athletic teams, Colgate has a diverse range of student organizations, from publications to event planning to cultural groups, among others.

Hookups or Relationships?

Hookups. Colgate is a school of extremes in the dating department, with fewer cases of people straddling the line. You can occassionally find couples sitting together at lunch, but much more prevalent are the random hookups that occur every weekend. Students tend to go out every night of the week, except Sunday and Tuesday. It is highly likely that they will meet someone that is interested in hooking up with them, but this attraction often fizzles by morning. Couples do exist, and those that actually reach that stage last for years, but more often, "relationships" only last for a couple hours. The problem with a small school is that there's not a lot of room to keep skeletons in the closet; it's nearly impossible to avoid anyone on this campus, so choose your "friends" carefully!

Best Place to Meet Guys/Girls

Fraternity parties and date parties between fraternities and sororities are great places to meet lots of different people. If you're not part of Greek life, people meet everywhere on campus; in dorm room parties, walking into town on their way to the bars, in class, and as members of student organizations and athletic teams.

Dress Code

Preppy. It ranges from American Eagle and Abercrombie & Fitch button-ups and khakis, to J.Crew chinos, pink Polo shirts, and Vera Bradley accessories.

Did You Know?

Top Places to Find Hotties:

1. The gym
2. The Jug
3. Parties

Top Places to Hook Up:

1. The Jug
2. Fraternity parties
3. In the dorms
4. Formals
5. Bars in general

Students Speak Out On...
Guys & Girls

"Many of the boys and girls at our school are fresh-faced and exercise regularly, and are thus quite physically attractive."

"For many, what might otherwise be considered hotness is unfortunately impeded by their self-imposed group mentality, and subsequent **tendency to look almost identical to the Polo sporting gangsta** beside them."

"**There's practically no dating scene** at Colgate, but the people are all good looking. Guys and girls alike seem to just be looking for weekend flings."

"The boys that are on campus are mostly very hot. The girls, if they are lucky enough to get one of the guys, are very protective, but **many of the girls have boyfriends anyway**."

"It's a really good-looking campus. I can remember taking my first tour of Colgate, and the group started out walking up the hill. I thought the first boy we passed was very good-looking. The next boy went by, and he was even better looking. **By the time we passed the fifth guy, even my mother was ready to apply**. The girls match the boys and are all very pretty. It is a campus of wealthy, in-shape, well-dressed, smart, and good-looking kids."

"I don't think we have a lot of hot guys. **People here are hot because of their brains, not their bodies**."

"My mom told me when I was applying to Colgate that it was the "**school of beautiful people**." I figured I'd make the judgment for myself when I actually saw the student body—she was right. A hub of athletic activity, most of the students are in good shape, and for the most part incredibly attractive. Look for popped collars on shirts and Ugg boots; the school is preppy, a typical Northeast university. Seriously, we're hot."

"**Everyone on the campus looks the same**. I can never remember whom I do and do not know. It's like a walking J.Crew catalogue. People dress alike, act alike, and think alike, for the most part. Different options and viewpoints are not really fostered. There are probably a total of five overweight people on the whole campus. Everyone flips their collars up, and boys really like pink pants. Some people think this sort of thing is hot and cool; I'm just not one of them."

"As put so well by Dennis Miller, '**You will never be so close to so many beautiful women that don't want to have anything to do with you**.' Actually, it is true—Colgate is full of gorgeous women that range from the psycho, rich bitch to the easy, nympho freaks in disguise, yet in some places this coalesces into an amazing person. Women come in all types, and it is best getting to actually know them, not just gawk and drool. Expect a lot of girls from the East and New England. All of my friends wanted to visit me, so that they could just look at the scenery as it walked by."

"**Sunny days at Colgate are a blessing**, but the snow hampers most of the short skirts and bare midriffs. These women seem willing to experience life finally not under their parents control, which leads to some wild nights and crazy stories. The women make amazing friends and seem more heterogeneous of a crowd than a lot of the guys do at times. A lot of the guys just seem to fit a lot of elitist stereotypes, but that is usual I suppose. I say meet everyone and just enjoy the view."

"People at Colgate are very good-looking—always jogging and stuff. But **most people just hook up**. Very few are into actually dating."

"Let's just say that I don't hear anyone complaining, ever. **Colgate is an extremely aesthetically-pleasing campus**, in terms of both the campus itself, and those who are on it."

"I am not sure whether there is something in the water, but Colgate, each of my four years there, was easily the **best-looking community I have ever seen**. Most of the people look as though they have just returned from a photo shoot for a J.Crew catalog."

"The students are great, **everyone is open minded** and a lot of fun to hang out with, and the girls are hot!"

"The guys are very nice and always play the '**I can take you home to Mom role**' like champs—even if they aren't really the best guys. When I was studying abroad last semester, I met a guy from George Washington, and when I told him I was from Colgate, he said, 'Wow, you are the first girl I met from Colgate who doesn't wear pearls.' So, I guess we have a reputation, too!"

"As for the women, it is impossible for me to imagine another part of the country with so many hot women in one place at one time. **If I could marry all of them, I would gladly switch my religious preferences**."

The College Prowler Take On...
Guys & Girls

The testimonies cannot be refuted. Colgate is a beautiful campus, regarding both the grounds and the students who attend it. Most everyone is wealthy, well-dressed, and fit. Sometimes it can be a bit overwhelming, like flipping through a J.Crew catalog, with guys sporting pink shorts and girls wearing their characteristic pearls to class. We think Colgate may have invented the flipped collar (or at least it feels that way sometimes), so the controversy over collars-up or collars-down ensues. And, of course, we Colgaters are hot—do you even need to ask?

In terms of dating, it happens, but one must remember that the students are 17–22-year-olds away from home with their own place to crash and booze at their disposal. The party scene complements the hookups that abound every weekend. Couples do date, but relationships for the most part are casual. More often than not, the case is either sexile your roommate, or be sexiled yourself.

The College Prowler® Grade on

Guys: A-

A high grade for Guys indicates that the male population on campus is attractive, smart, friendly, and engaging, and that the school has a decent ratio of guys to girls.

The College Prowler® Grade on

Girls: B+

A high grade for Girls not only implies that the women on campus are attractive, smart, friendly, and engaging, but also that there is a fair ratio of girls to guys.

The Lowdown On... Athletics

Athletic Division:
Division I for all sports, except for football, which is Division I-AA

Conference:
Patriot League

School Mascot
Raider

Males Playing Varsity Sports:
306 (22%)

Females Playing Varsity Sports:
248 (18%)

→

Men's Varsity Sports:

Basketball
Crew
Cross-Country
Diving
Field Hockey
Football
Golf
Ice Hockey
Lacrosse
Soccer
Swimming
Tennis
Track

Women's Varsity Sports:

Basketball
Crew
Cross-Country
Diving
Field Hockey
Ice Hockey
Lacrosse
Soccer
Softball
Swimming
Tennis
Track
Volleyball

Club Sports:

Aikido
Alpine Ski Team
Badminton

(Club Sports, continued)

Baseball
Cheerleading
Equestrian
Fencing
Field Hockey
Figure Skating
Fly Fishing
Golf (women)
Ice Hockey (men)
Ice Hockey (women)
Juggling
Lacrosse
Martial Arts
Rugby
Running
Sailing
Ski Club
Soccer
Squash
Ultimate Frisbee
Volleyball
Water Polo

Intramurals:

Basketball
3-on-3 Basketball
Bowling
Flag Football
4-on-4 Flag Football
Ice Hockey
Raquetball
Soccer
Softball
Tennis
Ultimate Frisbee
Volleyball

Athletic Fields

Andy Kerry Stadium: Football

Sanford Fieldhouse: Indoor Track and Field

Tyler's Field: Field Hockey and Lacrosse

Van Doren Field: Soccer

Getting Tickets

Tickets are easy to get. If students show their student ID, they enjoy free admission to regular season home games.

Most Popular Sports

The student body most avidly supports football (at least until the snow starts) and men's hockey. Large percentages of the student body come out to watch the Raiders play, not simply because they win, but also because they are close friends with many of the athletes.

Overlooked Teams

Every sport has its following. Because so many of last year's teams advanced to the Division I finals, they all received a great deal of support and attention from the students, staff, and administration of Colgate. Those that get less attention include the softball, volleyball, and crew teams.

Best Place to Take a Walk

Take a nice stroll down Willow Path and around Taylor Lake to see the famous pair of swans, Adam and Eve.

Jogging trails run above campus near the old golf course and across the old ski slopes.

A walk into town is always relaxing and fun.

Gyms/Facilities

Andy Kerr Stadium
The on-campus football stadium seats 10,221. The Frederick H. Dunlap East Stands were constructed in 1991.

Cotterell Court
Located in Reid Athletic Center and renovated in 2000, the court hosts volleyball and basketball games.

Eaton Street Complex
It serves as the practice grounds for Colgate's championship softball team.

The Glendening Boathouse
Recently completed in the spring of 2004, the boathouse is three miles from Colgate on Lake Moraine. Nearly 100 students a day utilize the facility's eight racing 8s, two novice training 8s, and two racing 4s.

Harry H. Lang Cross Country Course
A staple in the men's and women's cross-country workout, it is suited for both the men's 8K race and the women's 5K race.

Huntington Gymnasium
The main workout facility for most athletes and the general student body. A revamped workout and fitness complex occupies a large portion of the downstairs near the locker rooms, indoor Olympic swimming pool, sauna, and team practice rooms. Upstairs are the volleyball courts, basketball courts, racquetball courts, aerobics, and martial arts rooms.

J.W. Abrahamson Memorial Courts
Found next to Sanford Fieldhouse, it serves as an outdoor facility for Colgate's men's and women's tennis teams, with nine regulation clay courts.

Lineberry Natatorium
Found adjacent to Huntington Gym, it is home to one of the finest indoor-outdoor facilities of its kind in America. The building holds a 50-meter, L-shaped pool, including a 25-yard, eight-lane competition area. The natatorium uses changeable bulkheads and is one of two natatoriums with a retractable roof this side of the Mississippi River.

Peter Browning Track
Colgate's state-of-the-art, seven-lane, 400 meter, polyurethane all-surface track, complete with throwing and jumping areas, circles the football field in Andy Kerr Stadium.

Sanford Field HouseRaider Power Performance Center: Student-Athlete Training Center
Officially opened in September of 2000, the 5,5000 square foot, state-of-the-art performance center contains a 40-foot peaked ceiling with sky lights, large paned picture windows, and Astroturf flooring. It can accommodate 26 teams (over 600 athletes) daily. Its advanced weight machines and strength and toning machines are just next to the speed and agility training and testing machines, equipped with electronic timing systems.

Sanford Field House
The facility boasts one of the finest indoor practice facilities in the Northeast and Patriot League with its artificial surface. It houses tennis competitions, and provides an indoor facility for track, tennis, lacrosse, and soccer teams to practice during cold winter months.

Seven Oaks Golf Course
Seven Oaks Golf Course, a Robert Trent Jones championship course, is rated by *Golf Digest* among the top five college courses, and the seventh-best public access course in NY state.

William Brian Little Fitness Center
The newest addition to Huntington Gym, it houses the University's main workout facility. Its 9,000 square feet of workout space contains state-of-the-art equipment, and a juice bar is conveniently located just before one enters from the gym.

Students Speak Out On... Athletics

"Varsity sports are huge. We're Division I in everything, I-AA in football. We were the Patriot League champs in football, and have made it to the IAA National Championship game."

"Most of our teams end up seeing post-regular season action. Our hockey team has won the Patriot League championship, as well. **Hockey games are intense, especially against Cornell**, when basically the entire student body shows up to see the Raiders versus the Big Red. Women's basketball made it to the NCAA tournament recently, for the first time ever. Lacrosse is big, too. Our women's team has done incredibly well."

"Hockey, basketball, and football are fairly popular, but only with certain contingents. The only time a sport truly captures the attention of the campus is **when it is dominating its league**."

"Raider athletics are big. **We are one of the smallest** Division I schools, and everyone goes out to support our teams. A few years ago, the football team made it to the Division I-AA final game. Everyone was so psyched up. IM sports are huge, too. There is a great system set up, and like 80 percent of students participate at some point in their four years. IM sports range from traditional soccer and basketball, to trap shooting and bowling. Go Gate!"

"Sports are huge. There is a huge following for our championship teams. Tons of people turn out for football, basketball, hockey, and lax games. **Everyone on the campus stays active**, goes to the gym, or plays on an IM team."

"Sports are pretty popular. People like to go to football, basketball, and hockey games. A large percentage of those not involved in varsity sports play IM. There are so many sports to choose from, and **you can always start a team, if you have enough players**."

"Varsity sports are huge. **Most students are really supportive of the athletic teams**, especially football and hockey. I have a lot of friends who are on IM teams. It's really easy to put a team together and play whichever sport is in season. People get totally into it. It's actually really fun to watch!"

"Colgate is so unique, because we have the **close-knit community of a small liberal arts college**, but the resources and services of a large, public university. One of the areas Colgate excels in versus its peer schools is athletics. We have roughly 20 Division I varsity sports, and our teams don't just compete—they win. In past years, our football team competed in the Division I-AA national championship (televised on ESPN), our men's hockey team was nationally-ranked for much of the season (ahead of schools more than 10 times our size), and our women's basketball team made the NCAA tournament."

"**There is a ton of school spirit on campus**, and Colgate students enthusiastically support our athletic teams. The great thing about having successful sports teams at a small school like Colgate is that the athletes you watch on the playing field are the same people you recognize from one of your classes. The various levels of interaction both in and outside the classroom among students help personalize your experience on campus."

The College Prowler Take On...
Athletics

Athletic competition has always been an important aspect of Colgate tradition. In keeping with this tradition, Colgate is constantly revamping, remodeling, and renovating its workout facilities every year in response to the high frequency of students. All of its varsity teams are Division I, and their many championship titles merit recognition. Fittingly, students support Raider athletics whenever the opportunity arises. But there isn't as spirited a following as large southern universities or Big 10 schools have.

One cannot ignore the crowd of students who stand outside in a ten-degree blizzard to watch its championship football team, or the rambunctious mob of students who tore down a goal post after a Raider football victory. Hockey games always see enthusiastic and boisterous crowds, and students, along with other teams, support each other well.

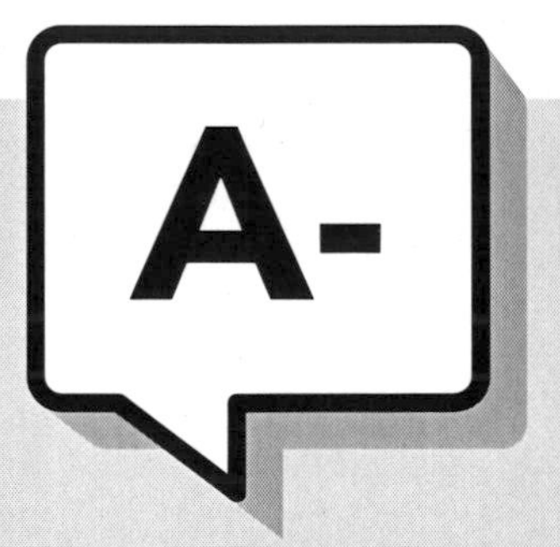

The College Prowler® Grade on

Athletics: A-

A high grade in Athletics indicates that students have school spirit, that sports programs are respected, that games are well-attended, and that intramurals are a prominent part of student life.

Nightlife

The Lowdown On... Nightlife

Club and Bar Prowler: Popular Nightlife Spots!

The Hourglass

20 Lebanon St.

(315) 824-8666

Frequented by upperclassmen looking for a drink and a chill time with their friends. It's not as crowded as the Jug, but still a good time if you're of age.

Nichols & Beal

10 Utica St.

(315) 824-2222

Restaurant during the day; bar at night. It's a bit classier than some and has a quieter crowd. More specialty drinks here than some others with its top-shelf liquor.

→

→

The Old Stone Jug

30 Utica St.

The "Jug" is packed Wednesday through Saturday night. This is the only bar where freshmen are permitted in; the other bars require two forms of 21-plus ID. Warning—it gets messy and very hot. Tie your jacket together with a friend's so that you do not lose it, and watch out for couples lip-locking in the corner.

The Tap Room at the Colgate Inn

1 Payne St.

(315) 824-2300

(The Tap Room, continued)

Classy like Nichols and Beal, it's popular on Thursday nights for cheap 50 cent drafts and live music performances.

Turning Stones Casino Resort

www.turningstone.com

5218 Patrick Rd
Verona, NY

(800) 771-7711

For the hopeful or hopeless. Go with a posse and have a fun time at the tables or playing cards. It's a change of pace from the regular bar hopping.

Primary Areas with Nightlife:

Downtown is the only place to go, hardly anyone ever ventures out of the town to Syracuse or other not-so-close universities.

Cheapest Place to Get a Drink:

Free at the frats unless the party is catered.

The Jug

Student Favorites:

The Glass (the Hour Glass)

The Old Stone Jug

Bars Close At:

2 a.m. or 2:30 a.m.

Favorite Drinking Games

Beirut

Flip Cup

Power Hour

Card Games

Quarters

Useful Resources for Nightlife:

AIM (AOL Instant Messenger)—it's your friend and lifeline

Word of mouth

What to Do if You're Not 21

- Hang out in your room or at the fraternity houses.
- The University works hard to provide an assortment of non-alcholic events, such as the regular take two film scenes that plays free flicks every weekend.

Organization Parties

Student organizations sometimes throw parties, but not as often as Greeks, or some theme houses. The best way to know about them is through campus distributions and e-mail. LASO usually sponsors a Latin Dance Party during the Fall, and there's also Broad Street Around the World, where theme houses provided students with food and drinks (alcoholic with proof of age) from different countries.

Frats

See the Greek section!

Students Speak Out On... Nightlife

"I think all I'm going to say about this one, is that Colgate is notorious for being a party school. Students work extremely hard, but they also party hard."

"**The frat parties are fun and always are crowded**, so you will always find people to hang out with even if you go out by yourself for the night. The Jug is the freshmen's favorite bar, and they won't hesitate to tell you. Everyone else loves it, too, but they will always deny it!"

"Parties are plentiful—**you can always find a party to go to** in student houses off campus, or in the frats on Broad Street. For the under-21 scene, The Old Stone Jug, referred to by students as 'the Jug' is our dance club, but also has a bar for students 21-and-over. The Palace is part of the community-based initiative between Colgate and the Hamilton community, and brings in a lot of small bands, other entertainment, and some dance scene."

"The **Hourglass** is a nice place to go and hang out."

"Sad to say, but the **party scene at Colgate is slowly dying**."

"Most things to do remain on campus or in student housing, fraternities, or apartments. **The Jug is infamous for being a good time**, as long as you don't stay sober."

"You never have had so much fun being packed in to a small room clustered around a table freshly unhinged, I must say. **Frat parties can be really great**, if you go with friends, and at least know someone there that can help you out with actually having fun. Cover fees suck pretty bad, so that is why learning to have a party in your own room, or in the hall, is the best part."

"Parties are usually always going on during the weekends, but eventually, if you look hard enough, **it is the Monday and Wednesday night room parties that are small and vibrant that make things best**. Meet your RA, become his or her friend, and learn what it takes to let him or her actually let you have a party on the entire floor. Clubs off campus—well if you like standing in the middle of an empty room with good music, then there is that. If you like standing pressed against a wall with people you can barely see and loud music you can't hear, then there is that, too. I would recommend a frat band party instead, where there is usually room and people are willing to be stupid and actually dance to have fun, instead of to get laid."

"On-campus parties usually are lots of fun, because **you actually get to know people**, but when it comes time for the cops to show up, just remember that it happens to everyone, and your parents will usually never find out."

"There are only three bars in the town of Hamilton. As an underclassman especially, **the social scene revolves around heavy drinking**, and can become redundant quickly. I would be concerned about the social options available for incoming freshmen."

The College Prowler Take On...
Nightlife

Despite the somewhat faltering social scene when compared to past years, Colgate students still know how to have a good time. They know how to balance academics and a good time—work really hard, so you can party even harder. First-years still feeling out of the party scene party mostly in the dorms, at least until 11:30 p.m., when they catch the shuttle (it's the "drunk bus" by night) to hit up the infamous Jug. As students age, partying moves from the dorms to the frats and bars. One never has to look far for a drinking buddy as at Colgate, Wednesday is the new Friday and Monday is the new Wednesday; in other words, nearly every night at Colgate is an excuse to go out.

However, if drinking, dancing, and chilling at the bars is not your cup of booze, look somewhere else. Students can enjoy quiet evenings at the Coop or staying in to watch a movie, but they cannot avoid the social scene forever. Colgate is a party campus despite the rigorous academics. Colgate students are always willing to drink and party, but some tire of the same frats and bars because there are no clubs nearby, and Syracuse is a bit of a hike for just one night of drinking.

The College Prowler® Grade on
Nightlife: B

A high grade in Nightlife indicates that there are many bars and clubs in the area that are easily accessible and affordable. Other determining factors include the number of options for the under-21 crowd and the prevalence of house parties.

The Lowdown On...
Greek Life

Number of Fraternities:
6

Number of Sororities:
4

Undergrad Men in Fraternities:
35%

Undergrad Women in Sororities:
32%

→

Fraternities on Campus:

Beta Theta Pi

Delta Upsilon

Phi Delta Theta

Phi Kappa Tau

Sigma Chi

Theta Chi

Sororities on Campus:

Delta Delta Delta

Gamma Phi Beta

Kappa Alpha Theta

Kappa Kappa Gamma

Other Greek Organizations:

Gamma Sigma Alpha (Greek Honors Society)

Greek Council

Greek Peer Advisors

Interfraternity Council (IFC)

Order of Omega

Panhellenic Council

Students Speak Out On...
Greek Life

"You can't go through recruitment until you're a sophomore, which is a really good thing. It forces you to get settled and make friends outside of a frat or sorority, before you decide to rush or pledge."

"You can make Greek life as much a part of your Colgate social scene as you want it to be. **I've never had a problem getting into a frat party**, but I feel like there are plenty of other options if I don't want to go to a party during the weekend."

"**I have enjoyed my time** in the Greek community, but it does not dominate the social scene."

"It doesn't dominate, but **it is a prominent option**. All Greek events are open to the campus and are very welcoming. Unfortunately, the school has been in a battle with the Greek houses. The school wishes to acquire the houses completely, while the fraternities prefer a lease option that will assure their continued existence in houses they built, in most cases, over 80 years ago. This conflict will be heating up over the next year."

"By the time this is published, I hope there is still some Greek life left at Colgate. The administration has come up with a very aggressive 'curb-the-fraternities policy,' and **it is sucking the lifeblood out of the social scene** here at Colgate. However, as long as Greek life is around, one thing is for sure, not many days will pass without incident."

"I must say that **Greek life dominates the social scene**, until you meet enough people that you can rebel and just hang out in a room drinking. Truthfully, what matters is individual preference—for me, no; for lots of people, yes. It all depends on what you consider fun, and what you think defines a frat. Make friends or buy them, you just have to pick. Frats open up a lot of opportunities, but you can just as easily talk to people in class and around campus. Greek life is what you want it to be in your life. Spring Party Weekend, though; there is nothing like Greek life at that point.

"Greek life is, I believe, an important aspect of Colgate, but it does not dominate the social scene. **The freshmen are somewhat alienated from Greek life**; either they know no members of fraternities or sororities, or they spend all their time tying to impress a brother or sister, in the hopes that they will be given a bid sophomore year. As upperclassmen, non-Greeks will attend parties while generally satisfied that they did not 'go Greek.' As upperclassmen, Greeks will invite non-Greek friends to their parties, but they generally become focused on their fraternity or sorority, and lose touch with those friends outside of their house."

"**Greek life does not dominate the social scene**, but without it, the campus would just be a series of small parties held by the same groups of people, inviting the same individuals."

"Greek life does kind of dominate the social scene, but I think that there really is **an organization for everyone if they want to join**. Joining an organization opens up so many more social options, which you're definitely ready for by sophomore year."

The College Prowler Take On...
Greek Life

Greek life is an important part of Colgate tradition, but unfortunately, like many Northeastern universities, the college is making motions to lessen the presence of the Greek system on campus. According to upperclassmen who reminisce about the good ol' days, when several frats hosted parties every week, this is working. Fraternities and sororities do continue to provide a great deal of social options and opportunities for friendship. All the Greek groups at Colgate also hold several philanthropic events annually.

Some students who join Greek houses become fully immersed in their organization, either because of leadership positions, or because they feel better connected with their new friends. Other students attend their Greek functions but maintain close connections with their pre-recruitment friends. Many students enter recruitment simply to pump up their social lives; others seem more committed to creating a positive Greek experience for all involved parties. Those who join Greek organizations, for the most part, do not regret their decisions. They enjoy a house, a whole new set of friends or acquaintances, and a whole other world of social options, but these do not come without a fee. However, Greek life at Colgate is not as expensive as at other schools, and students cannot join an organization until their sophomore year. This leads to a mostly pleasant balance between going Greek but not becoming totally sucked into the scene.

The College Prowler® Grade on

Greek Life: A

A high grade in Greek Life indicates that sororities and fraternities are not only present, but also active on campus. Other determining factors include the variety of houses available and the respect the Greek community receives from the rest of the campus.

Drug Scene

The Lowdown On...
Drug Scene

Most Prevalent Drugs on Campus:

Alcohol
Marijuana

Liquor-Related Referrals:

343

Liquor-Related Arrests:

0

Drug-Related Referrals:

159

Drug-Related Arrests:

4

Drug Counseling Programs:

Confidential drug, alcohol, and health counseling services are provided at the Conant House.

Students Speak Out On... Drug Scene

"I've gotta say, the only thing I know about drugs on campus is what I've heard. Marijuana is popular. I haven't ever found drugs to be an issue."

"The drug scene can be summed up by saying '**most have tried it; few do it regularly**.' Marijuana has been smoked by a majority of Colgate students, but few are regular smokers. Other drugs, such as psychedelic mushrooms and cocaine, are taken much less frequently by a far smaller number of students. Drugs such as Adderall are common, but not taken for recreational purposes."

"**Nearly all Colgate students drink**, and nearly all of them drink to get drunk. Alcohol is readily available and regularly abused. I do not believe that the amount of drinking on this campus is a problem specific to Colgate, but for those individuals who do not drink (or even do not drink to get drunk), the social scene is much more limited."

"Marijuana is there if you want it. Adderall or Ritalin is also there if you want it. Cocaine and opium are there if you are willing to look for it. 'Shrooms are there if you want them. You will learn to get along with people drinking, smoking, or getting high in most situations, as you learn to feel out what is socially acceptable and what isn't. You could be very creative in learning how to make bongs or pipes. **Stress relief takes on many different forms**."

"There is **a lot of underage drinking** and minor pot usage."

"A lot of people smoke pot at Colgate, but I don't think there are many problems with hard drugs. **Drinking is, of course, the main drug of choice** for Colgate students."

"It's definitely here, but it's definitely not everyone's thing. **Most kids drink a lot freshman year**, but beyond that, the drug use is pretty minimal until they become upperclassmen. It's definitely something you can choose to get into, but there are many who do not."

The College Prowler Take On...
Drug Scene

Like most other college campuses, drugs are part of the scene, but at Colgate, they are not a major problem. There are the regulars who smoke up weekly or more often, but the most common drug is alcohol, not narcotics. If people do smoke, they do it quietly, not blatantly; doors are closed, windows are opened, and fans are switched on.

Drug-related referrals and arrests have increased in the last four years, but seem to be balancing out now. People who choose to be foolish about their drug use are more likely to make this list, whereas those who are smart and discrete with their drug use will get away with it. Alcohol related arrests and referrals are much more popular. It is quite easy to find marijuana, but users are quite considerate for the most part. Harder drugs are nowhere near as visible and do not pose a threat to most students.

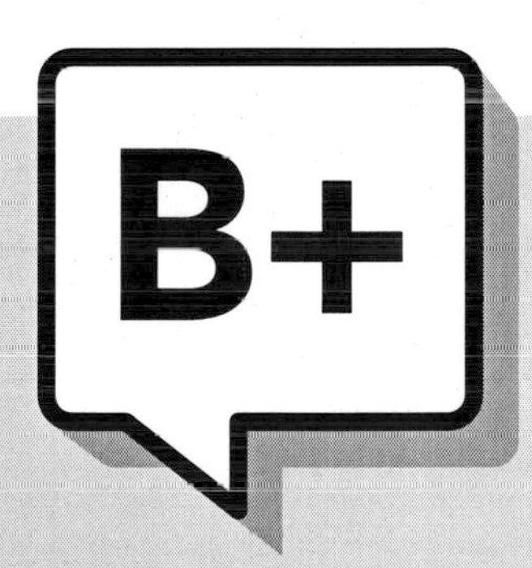

The College Prowler® Grade on

Drug Scene: B+

A high grade in the Drug Scene indicates that drugs are not a noticeable part of campus life; drug use is not visible, and no pressure to use them seems to exist.

Campus Strictness

The Lowdown On... Campus Strictness

What Are You Most Likely to Get Caught Doing on Campus?

Smoking pot

Students Speak Out On...
Campus Strictness

"The less said about Campus Safety (or "Campo," as they are lovingly known), the better. Let's say they are not very tolerant of students."

"**Campus Safety is strict about drugs**, and students who are caught with them are punished accordingly, but when it comes to drinking, students are mostly just written up and required to meet with a Residential Education staff member. After three write-ups in a semester, the punishment becomes more severe, but for the most part, students are able to have their fun without being out of control."

"Campus police are generally okay with drinking and drugs. They know what goes on at the Jug and at frat parties, but **they give a lot of leniency**. However, if you are caught with alcohol or pot, expect to face some sort of disciplinary action. Usually, though, this amounts to a slap on the wrist, and I know of no individuals who gave up drinking or smoking after an encounter with Campus Safety. "

"**You get a slap on the wrist, basically**. Just don't get caught smoking out, otherwise you might actually get in a little trouble. In such an isolated campus with often so little to do, drugs seems to have become a recognized, if even at times tolerated, way of recreation. Alcohol is a drug to everyone."

"Campo is strict about the drinking that they catch going on, although first offense punishments are not too serious. Getting caught underage with alcohol or drugs is very different on a college campus than in the real world. The policies are not as stringent (**you won't go to jail** or pay court ordered fines for possession), but they still do make an effort to patrol and minimize big parties on campus (not that they succeed)."

"The policies are strict, but **it is not difficult to get away** with certain things on campus."

"**They are pretty lenient**. You usually get a warning at least, before you get into big trouble about both alcohol and marijuana."

"As for drinking, they usually won't bother you, as long as you're not drinking in the open. **If you do get caught** with that kind of stuff, you just have to go to alcohol and drug classes. Not really a big deal."

The College Prowler Take On... Campus Strictness

Campus Safety, though visible on campus, does not intimidate most students. The most common thing to be nailed for is drinking or marijuana use. Once students feel out their RAs and Campus Safety, they know how to avoid getting caught drinking in their room or partying. Students are allowed three offenses before a counseling referral and are sometimes punished by changing dormitories. Even so, most students rarely experience disciplinary action, and if they do, they soon forget about it, and their lifestyles are in no way altered. Just don't make it a habit of getting caught, because what starts as a warning can eventually turn into more severe repercussions for repeat offenders.

Campus Safety exist for the safety of students and tend to let quite a bit slide. If you make them take action, such as making a scene or getting caught with possession of alcohol or marijuana, then they will take the appropriate action. Despite the regular patrols by either officers or students, Campus Safety does not impose a threat on student activities. However, they do maintain some visibility, in order to make students feel that they are still watched and protected.

The College Prowler® Grade on

Campus Strictness: A-

A high Campus Strictness grade implies an overall lenient atmosphere; police and RAs are fairly tolerant, and the administration's rules are flexible.

The Lowdown On... Parking

Approximate Parking Permit Cost:
Free

Common Parking Tickets:
No Parking Zone: $25
Handicapped Zone: $50
Fire Lane: $50

Student Parking Lot?
The freshman parking lot is in front of Tyler's Field at the bottom of the hill, and the Cutten parking lot next to the Cutten Housing Complex. There are also various small parking lots by the Birch and Parker apartments, and by Greek and theme houses.

Freshmen Allowed to Park?
Yes

Colgate Parking Services

The main parking lot is the freshman lot next to Starr Rink and in front of Tyler's field. Trying to get a spot by the road is somewhat difficult, but not horrible. However, it is still a trek up the hill during freshman year. Sophomores may park in the Cutten parking lot after 3:30 p.m. during the weekdays and on the weekends. Seniors living off campus are allowed to park their cars in the Cutten Lot, and along Lally Lane, before classes during the day. Overnight parking is not allowed unless with permission, but Campus Safety is sometimes lenient over the weekends. During the winter, Campus Safety tows vehicles that are parked after 3 a.m., and charges the owner a $75 towing fee. Cars are not allowed up the hill past the roundabout by the Curtis clock until after 3:30 pm on weekdays.

Parking Permits

Acquiring parking permits is easy. Simply drive to Campus Safety with your license and registration, inform them of your needs, fill out the information card, and apply the decal to your vehicle. Permits are free.

Did You Know?

Best Places to Find a Parking Spot

The freshman parking lot early to late afternoon. Do not wait until right before you go to bed to get a parking spot; if you do, you will be parking in the back by Tyler's field.

Good Luck Getting a Parking Spot Here!

Next to Starr Rink

Students Speak Out On...
Parking

"It's easy to park if you live off campus or in the apartments because you can park right in front of your home. However, freshmen and sophomores living on campus have to park their cars in a student lot."

"**Parking up the hill is very limited**, so those small lots are reserved for faculty and staff until classes are over for the day. The 'freshman lot,' as it has been named, isn't a far walk from the freshman dorms, and it's even closer to the sophomore dorms. People complain a bit during the winter, but it's really not bad at all."

"Parking on campus is limited and can become **expensive if you pile up those tickets**."

"When you live in the dorms, parking isn't easy. The lot is about a mile away from most of the freshman dorms. It gets easier when students move downtown into apartments or college houses, though, because the parking lot is right in the backyard. **The good thing is that parking is free**, unless you get a lot of tickets! You can't drive up the hill and park to go to class, because you can't park on the hill until after all classes end, so even if you do have a car, you have to get someone to drop you off; you can't drive yourself."

"No, **it is not easy to get parking**—parking sucks. The lot is so far away, that it's really not even worth it to have a car your first year."

"I have no clue because **I don't have a car**. I am told it is a hike and a half to actually be able to get to the campus from your car. Parking sucks for the most part, especially during the winter, with all the ice and snow."

The College Prowler Take On... Parking

Parking is a pain your freshman year. It lets up considerably afterwards. Freshmen live up the hill, and the parking lot is at the very bottom, which leads to a very annoying, uphill hike, especially when it's 20 degrees and icy. We advise befriending dormmates with cars to personally avoid this as much as possible. As a sophomore, the parking lot appears much closer, and that is when a vehicle of your own comes in handy. Many sophomores park overnight in the Cutten Lot on the weekends, although there seems to be no predictable pattern as to whether or not this will result in a ticket. As a junior and senior, a parking lot is just seconds outside of your house or apartment. Be careful of overnight parking on the side of the road (as opposed to within designated spaces) because Campus Safety will ticket you, and you would much rather spend that money on things other than parking fines.

The freshman lot is really far away when you first get to school, but you get used to the hills, and nothing in Colgate is really more than a 15-minute walk. But you have to take all of these things into consideration and evaluate if it is even worth it to have a car on campus.

The College Prowler® Grade on

Parking: B-

A high grade in this section indicates that parking is both available and affordable, and that parking enforcement isn't overly severe.

Transportation

The Lowdown On... Transportation

Ways to Get Around Town:

On Campus

Colgate Cruiser

The Cruiser runs 7 a.m. to 2 a.m. generally, but its shuttle stops vary. Make sure to check the Cruiser Schedule, which is distributed to students and posted online. Also, the Cruiser always takes a break between 5 p.m. and 5:30 p.m.

Car Rentals

Avis
local: (800) 331-1212
national: (800) 831-2847
www.avis.com

Budget
local: (800) 527-0700
national: (800) 527-0700
www.budget.com

Enterprise
local: (800) 325-8007
national: (800) 736-8222
www.enterprise.com

Hertz
local: (800) 654-3131
national: (800) 654-3131
www.hertz.com

→

(Car Rentals continued)

National
local: (800) 227-7368
national: (800) 227-7368
www.nationalcar.com

Best Ways to Get Around Town

Walk – the most you will walk is fifteen or twenty minutes at a slow, leisurely pace

Wait for the cruiser

Ride with a friend in your car or theirs

Ways to Get Out of Town:

Airport

Syracuse Hancock International Airport

How to Get to the Airport

During Thanksgiving and winter break, the Colgate Student Travel Agency offers tickets for a shuttle going to and from the airport. Tickets are $20 one-way and $30 round trip. Students also arrange for a cab, but most generally ask a friend with a car to drive them.

Century Transportation has an exclusive agreement to provide ground transportation for Syracuse Hancock Int'l Airport.

(Century Transportation, continued)

For questions regarding ground transportation at Syracuse Hancock International Airport, contact the Department of Aviation at (315) 454-3263.

A cab ride to the airport costs $40.

Airlines Serving Syracuse

American Airlines
(800) 433-7300
www.americanairlines.com

Continental
(800) 525-0280
www.continental.com

Delta
(800) 221-1212
www.delta-air.com

JetBlue
(800) 538-2583
www.jetblue.com

Northwest
(800) 225-2525
www.nwa.com

United Express
(800) 241-6522
www.united.com

US Airways
(800) 428-4322
www.usairways.com

TransMeridian
(866) 435-9862
www.transmeridian-airlines.com

Travel Agents

Colgate Student Travel Agency

Center for Leadership and Student Involvement

Students Speak Out On...
Transportation

"It's awesome. The Colgate Cruiser takes you all around campus and town. It can be off schedule on occasion, which is frustrating, but for the most part, it's so great to have."

"**Students who live off campus and in the apartments can take the Cruiser up the hill** before class every morning. On Wednesday, Friday, and Saturday the Cruiser runs until 3:30 a.m. for students who are out and need a ride back to their dorms, so that no one drives after they've been drinking."

"Like all transportation, **it is always there when you don't need it**, but always late when you do. It's convenient, but always full at night. You will puke on it at some point; that is a given."

"The Colgate Cruiser (**known more widely as the 'drunk bus' for its weekend, late-night shuttling**) is very useful to get around campus, and more likely, off campus to town."

"The Colgate Cruiser is pretty convenient, although you may be waiting in the snow for a long time before it shows up. **It beats walking home or getting a DUI**."

"The Cruiser is usually pretty dependable. It runs frequently and **generally stops for you when you're running after it**."

"**The Crusier (by day), the drunk bus (by night)** is really convenient, and if you live up on the hill, you use it a lot. It really helps to prevent drunk driving at night, and it's really useful for going to the bookstore and the grocery store downtown during the day."

The College Prowler Take On...
Transportation

There is basically one way to get to Colgate, and that is by car—either being picked up by a friend, driving one's own car, or paying for a taxi. Some take the train from Utica, which is an hour away, others may take a Greyhound from Binghamton, but a car is the most efficient and convenient form of transportation to and from our small-town campus. On campus, students walk everywhere, so get used to the hills. Colgate allows first-years to bring vehicles to campus, but the parking lot is relatively far.

Many students wait at shuttle stops to take the Cruiser, but about the same number would rather walk than wait, because nothing on campus is more than a 15-minute walk. The Cruiser is relatively reliable—just make sure you know the schedule, in case it's on its break between 5 and 5:30 pm. It's no fun waiting on the Cruiser, especially in the dead of winter when temperatures plummet below freezing. The Cruiser is reliable, and perfect for students who are drunk, cold, or just plain lazy. In general, Colgate students are friendly, so it's usually easy to catch a ride. If not, our campus is small, so no walk is too bad. The main steps are heated to stay ice-free.

The College Prowler® Grade on

Transportation: B-

A high grade for Transportation indicates that campus buses, public buses, cabs, and rental cars are readily-available and affordable. Other determining factors include proximity to an airport and the necessity of transportation.

The Lowdown On... Weather

Average Temperature:	
Fall:	56 °F
Winter:	33 °F
Spring:	52 °F
Summer:	76 °F

Average Precipitation:	
Fall:	3.94 in.
Winter:	3.07 in.
Spring:	3.54 in.
Summer:	3.68 in.

Students Speak Out On... Weather

"A better question would be, 'what isn't the weather like?' It's hot at the beginning of the year, but come winter, you better bring every warm layer you own, and throw in a pair of boots as well."

"Fortunately, since it's such a small campus, **you're very rarely outside more than ten minutes at a time**. And, there's always the Cruiser if you need to get around town. Winters can be rough, but students have fun stealing trays from the cafeteria and sledding down the hill, or building snow sculptures in the quad, or sometimes just throwing snowballs at each other. There are definitely ways to have a good time, even in the cold!"

"You have to love the cold to come to Colgate. No matter how many times one lives through a Hamilton winter (which lasts six months), you will never get used to them. It gets cold enough in the thick of winter that people just don't go outside. **The weather really depresses the general mood** on campus during the winter months, but it also allows you to focus on getting your work done. When the weather finally gets warm, everyone immediately cheers up and hangs out outside. I have never seen people appreciate a partly sunny, 60-degree day more in my life than at Colgate."

"**It's cold, cold, cold**. Bring sweaters, coats, boots, jackets, snow pants, a sled, and some more coats."

"**Is it still snowing**? I think so!"

"Bring lots of cold weather gear, comfortable pajamas that you can wear while you stroll the halls or attend class, shoes that aren't hard to put on, waterproof coats that are nice and warm, and two pairs of sneakers, so that you can actually wear clean shoes in the gym. Jeans, T-shirts, and sweaters will be your friend. **Bring anything that stays clean easily and you don't mind wearing for more than a week**. Of course, bring the nice duds, too, when you want to be a big pimp at the party. Dress nice on occasion, and hell, bring a suit, too, because you never know when you have to look nice at a formal."

"The weather at first is beautiful and perfect, then chilly and artic for five months, then it is still too cold, becoming almost decent, then beautiful, and then the school year ends. It is easy to say you will learn that you can actually fall into a snow bank and disappear. **Be prepared to miss the sun**, too. Coming from a city where the sun is out 300 days a year, Colgate is one hell of a shock to a person not prepared."

"**Hmm, a parka**? Yeah, winter goes from about October until late April, but you'll never appreciate the sun more when it comes out for the first time. The icy winters just make spring and summer that much better!"

"It gets cold—really, really cold. **Bring a nice, heavy coat**, and you are all set."

The College Prowler Take On... Weather

The weather is cold, but not impossible. The snow is very beautiful when it gets as cold as it does in Hamilton, but it does not keep the students from enjoying their stay at the University. It is true, though, that once the snow starts to fall in October, it will not leave the campus for after six months, in April. Because of this long winter, mild depression can set in, and one should stay active and busy, in order to avoid getting stuck in a rut.

Bring lots of clothing with which to layer, because the walk to an early class can be bitterly cold with the wind, but professors may keep classrooms toasty. Down comforters and electric and fleece blankets are great ways to keep warm on a cold winter's night. Students sport NorthFace fleeces and Columbia ski jackets in addition to the classic pea coats from J.Crew and Banana Republic, equally popular. However, when the sun starts to shine and the snow starts to melt, mini-skirts and sunbathing are just around the corner, even if it is only 60 degrees outside. It is incredibly cold during the winter, but students do not find that it hampers their activities, or reduces their enjoyment of the school.

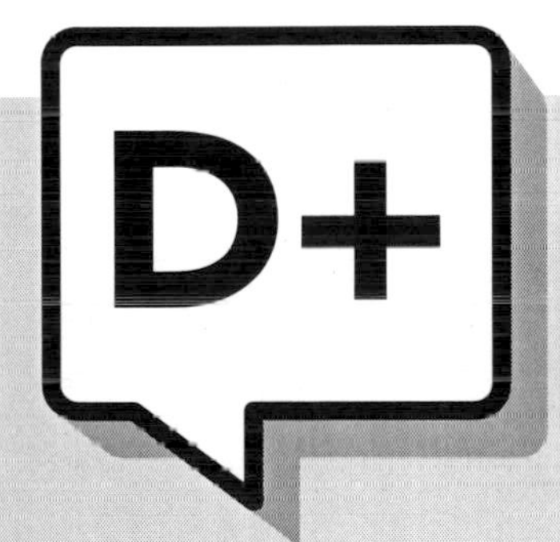

The College Prowler® Grade on

Weather: D+

A high Weather grade designates that temperatures are mild and rarely reach extremes, that the campus tends to be sunny rather than rainy, and that weather is fairly consistent rather than unpredictable.

COLGATE UNIVERSITY

Report Card Summary

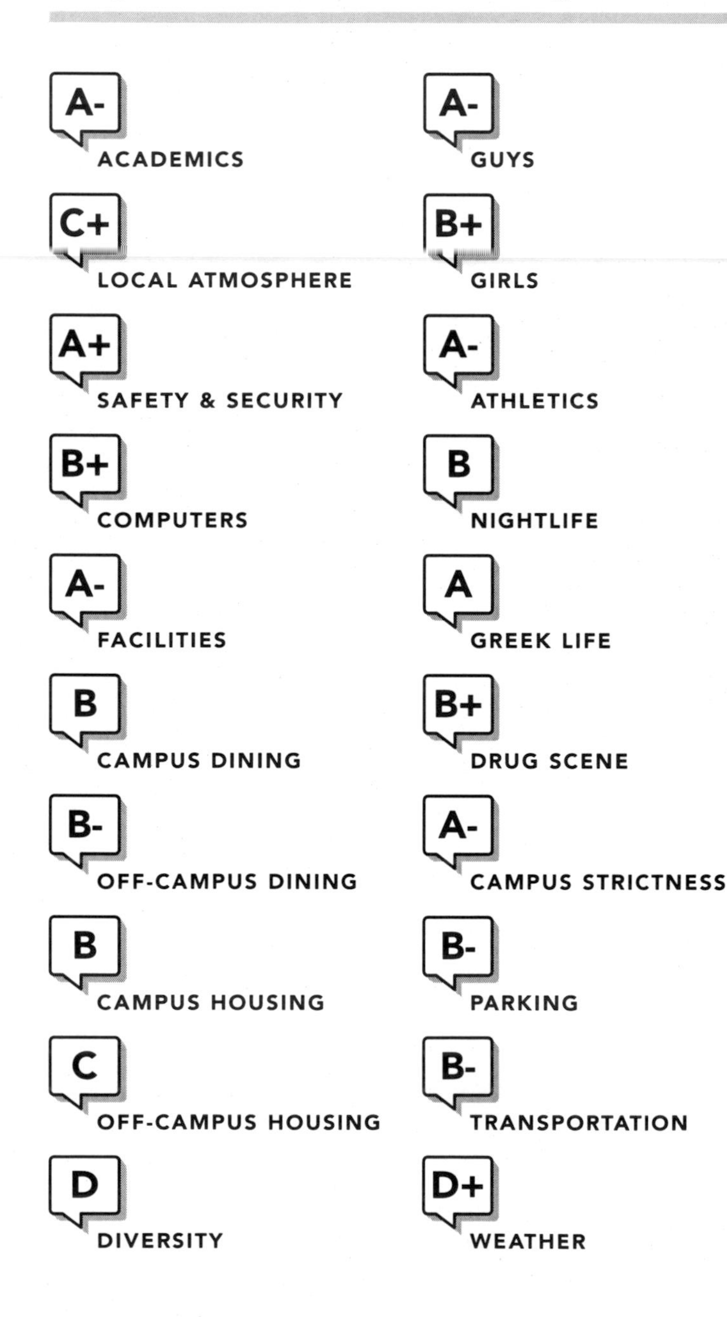

Overall Experience

Students Speak Out On... Overall Experience

"I love Colgate. It's a perfect fit for me. I just wish I didn't only have two years left! It's been an incredible experience—the people, the classes, the teachers, the activities, and the entertainment."

"Trying to decide on a college was possibly the most miserable few months of high school for me. I was absolutely torn between Colgate and Rutgers, for so many different reasons. Finally, I just went with my gut and chose Colgate. I've been here two years now, and **I couldn't even imagine being anywhere else**."

"**I love Colgate**, and I have no regrets of coming to this school."

"So far, I have really enjoyed my time at Colgate. I have experienced some of the best times of my life, and some of the toughest. While I never thought Colgate would be the quasi-elitist party school that it is, it has given me the opportunity to experience a life that I have never encountered before in southern New Jersey. If college is the time in your life to have fun, party, and put in only as much effort as you like, then Colgate is the perfect place. However, I have noticed over the past two years that **I am much more inquisitive and intelligent now than I was before I arrived in Hamilton, New York**. I have thus far received an excellent education and met some of the greatest people I have ever known, and would not trade this experience for any Ivy League institution or state institution closer to a major city."

"The opportunities and freedom one has to shape his or her college experience at Colgate makes it a great undergraduate experience. We have the academics of an Ivy League school, but a student body that can better balance their books with their beer. The community-driven, personal nature of the college makes each student's college career unique but similar. As a result, I think most students graduate from Colgate **feeling an intimate connection with all of their classmates**, and those that came before them. It is truly a special place."

"I love Colgate, and I don't think I would be anywhere else. I think I've developed more as a person in these past two years than I had for the first 18 years of my life. **I'll be very sad to leave Colgate**. I have made some amazing friends. Here is some advice—don't just come here because Colgate is in the academic elite of America. Come here because you will meet some of the most amazing people."

"The best part about Colgate is the size. **Nearly all classes have less than 40 students**, and in my first two years, all but two have been under 35 students, and a handful have been less than 15. The size allows you to approach professors with questions since they are required to have office hours, and no classes will be taught by TAs or graduate students. Additionally, the size of the school allows anyone to become very involved in many aspects of student life in event planning. It's very common that sophomores and juniors are running programs for music, lectures, and cultural events. The size allows you to see people you know all the time, while still seeing people you don't know all the time. Simply put, it's perfect."

"It's hard to get used to, but a blast once you have warmed up to **cold weather, eccentric people, high intelligence, and isolation**. The school is full of surprises and clichés at the same time. There are kids who drive a Mercedes everywhere and fly to Europe when they get bored, but there are always financial aid kids who hang out in the library, because they don't have their own computer—it's a hell of a place. It's an amazing place once you have learned to love it, and you are able to meet people that will make your life that much fuller. Take the pains with the pleasure, and wash it down with alcohol while your buddy carries you home from a blowout party, just enjoy your time in the la-la land of Colgate. I was told that after surviving Colgate, I could be dropped in the middle of Siberia, and I would find a way to cope and have fun."

"I love Colgate! **I wish I could stay here for more than four years**."

"**Colgate is my love**. I chose it over all the other critically acclaimed universities that accepted me because when I visited, the students seemed overwhelmingly happier here than at any other institution."

 "Sometimes I do wish I were somewhere else, but then I remember that **Colgate is an experience unlike any other**, and I have the rest of my life to live in a city and be surrounded by people with a grasp on reality. For now, I'm enjoying the dream world that is the snow globe of Hamilton, NY."

The College Prowler Take On...
Overall Experience

Simply put, Colgate students love Colgate. Prospective students pick Colgate as much as Colgate picks them. It is no surprise that the University's retention rate from freshman to sophomore year is 94 percent. It is the best combination of a small liberal arts college and a major university. It has the strong sense of community and warmth of a small college, but the impressive faculty and staff of a major university. Students have a variety of activities to choose from, such as student-run organizations and publications, clubs, and athletic teams. Whatever their interest, Colgate students find their niche and flourish. The University fosters growth and maturity, but most important is the amazing group of individuals living in the dorms and on staff.

Through all the partying and camaraderie, academics and organizations, Colgate grooms its students to become outstanding individuals, soon to be pillars of communities. Students love Colgate, and once you get past the weather, you should be fine. Most students never consider transferring. Their pride and enthusiasm for the school are contagious, and this sucks anyone in who was not convinced from the beginning.

The Inside Scoop

The Lowdown On... The Inside Scoop

Colgate Slang:

Know the slang, know the school. The following is a list of things you really need to know before coming to Colgate. The more of these words you know, the better off you'll be.

7000 – Colgate's phone directory, which allows you to type in a student's first and last name in order to call their room—an ingenious device.

Adam and Eve – The swans found gliding across Taylor lake every spring and fall.

ALANA Cultural Center – African, Latin, Asian, and Native American Cultural Center; organization and the building in which it is housed, that encourages the educating of students on multi-cultural issues.

The Annex – The motel-looking building behind the Theta sorority house.

The BAC – Budget Allocation Committee; student committee that allocates funds to all student organizations.

The Barge – A University-owned coffee house found on Broad Street across from the bookstore.

B&G – Buildings and Grounds; men and women who care for University facilities and grounds. Be nice to them. They lift and loft beds and clean your bathrooms.

Beverly and Jean – The two main ladies who swipe your 'Gate card and allow you to enter Frank. Make friends with them so that they will let you in when you forget your card.

Big M – Renamed Wayne's Market; small grocery store where many a booze is bought.

Birch – University Court Apartments, the dark blue apartments closest to Broad St.

CAB – Colgate Activities Board; student organization that schedules and plans entertainment acts who come to Colgate and publicize large student activities.

Case – Everett Needham Case Library (main library).

The Commons – Structure located in the center of Parker Apartments where juniors and seniors study and do their laundry; also home to many social events throughout the year.

Cooley – The Cooley Science library, located in the basement floor of McGregory Hall.

The Coop – Newly renovated O'Connor Campus Center, home to the stir-fry and deep-fry grill, amazing loafers, a Freshen's Yogurt and Smoothie Bar, CSLI (Center for Student Leadership and Involvement), the C-Store, the campus mailing center, a computer lab, and University Printing. It is the main dining choice of upperclassmen. Equipped with a wireless Internet network, one very large fireplace, another smaller fireplace, and some very nice plasma TVs.

The Cruiser – Commonly referred to as the "drunk bus," shuttles students up and down the hill and into town; a welcomed sight on cold winter nights.

The C-Store – Convenience store found on the main level of the Coop; home to lots of candies and miscellaneous items, but beware because you pay for the convenience.

D-Board – Disciplinary board.

The Edge – Dining hall connected to the Bryan Complex; great for Belgian waffles and "early" weekend breakfasts.

→

Frank – The Curtis E. Frank Dining Hall, main mecca of first year socializing.

Gate – Affectionate term for Colgate University.

The 'Gates – The Swinging 'Gates, Colgate's all female, a capella singing group.

Goosebeak – Charred Goosebeak; student improvisational comedy group—very funny.

The Hill – Colgate's main campus containing most academic buildings and first-year dormitories.

The HOP – Hall of Presidents; found in the Student Union down the hill above Donovan's Pub.

HRC – Harlem Renaissance Center; located in the Bryan Complex.

Inky – *Incunabulum*, first-year face book; never lose it! You will be looking up your classmates, and people you meet at the bars for years to come in this very helpful tool.

ITS – Information Technology Services; a group of staff and students with special knowledge and training; they help with all your computer needs, questions, and emergencies. If they can't help you, keep trying and asking around. Someone in the staff will know the answer to your problem.

Things I Wish I Knew Before Coming to Colgate

- Get to know your professors, and visit them during their office hours. They want you to stop by, and they'll like you more for it.
- Learn to balance studies and parties. Colgate is an amazing institution. Take advantage of the illustrious faculty. Still, these are some of the best years of your life, have fun and live without regrets.
- Form study groups and find study partners. Studying is more fun when you know you are not alone, and there are others to help you get through it.
- Get involved! There is an abundance of activities and organizations that satisfy all interests one can imagine. If you cannot find your niche, start a group. Colgate has lots of funding and encourages students to be active and independent.
- Be open to making new friendships. A wide variety of people attend Colgate. You will probably never get to meet such a diverse group of people in your life other than at school.
- Take advantage of Career Services and the alumni network. Some of the best opportunities are just waiting to be snatched up.

Colgate Urban Legends

Under the Deep

When Fiji lost its Charter after the Drug Olympics, the brothers threw all their furniture into Taylor Lake.

Raider PC

Colgate's Raider mascot was actually a Pirate, not a Native American, but the school decided to change its mascot from the Red Raiders to Raiders in the early 1990s to be politically correct.

School Spirit

With a student body that loves its school as much as Colgate's does, it is no surprise that the students, for the most part, exude a remarkable amount of school spirit for such a small institution. Many come out for athletic contests, such as football and hockey, and support their friends in less intense sports, like IM softball. Students are not apathetic, though some may exhibit more pride than others. Some become tour guides; others work in the admissions office, or student leadership office. Whenever students travel, they proudly sport their "Gate gear" and almost always run into alumnae in the far corners of the globe. Even as graduates, students never forget their ties to Colgate, which is one reason why the alumni base is so helpful in job placement.

Traditions

Thirteen

The Baptist Education Society of the State of New York and Colgate University was founded by thirteen men. Each offered $13 and thirteen prayers, and the Society's Constitution contained thirteen articles. Colgate has been non-sectarian since 1938. The first two digits in Colgate's zip code are thirteen and the last three numbers add up to thirteen (13346), the area code is 315, with a backwards thirteen inside.

The Diploma, Seal, and Motto

In 1846, Professors A. C. Kendrick and J. F. Richardson prepared the Latin formula for the diplomas that has remained intact ever since. They, along with Professor John Howard Raymond and three trustees, devised the seal and motto, "Deo Ac Veritati" ("With reference to God and for the purpose of truth," or simply "For God and for truth").

Salmagundi

The current name of Colgate's yearbook. The first volume of the *Salmagundi* was published by the Junior Class in 1883. The word means "miscellany" or "medley," and originally, the book contained lists of faculty, fraternities, other campus organizations and their respective members. Salmagundi became the yearbook for the graduating class in 1934.

Torchlight

The first senior Torchlight ceremony was held at Taylor Lake in 1930. On graduation night, the Colgate conducts a processional around the lake.

Hello Tradition

For decades, Colgate has had a wonderful "hello" tradition. Students, faculty, and staff walking on campus routinely say hello to a passerby. It's a way of getting to know others and welcoming strangers to campus.

First Kiss

Legend has it that whomever you kiss on the bridge where Willow Path crosses Taylor Lake is whom you will eventually marry. Maybe this why the number of married Colgate couples is higher than most university numbers.

Finding a Job or Internship

The Lowdown On... Finding a Job or Internship

Two of Colgate's biggest assets are its alumni base and its strong Center for Career Services. The staff at the Center are genuinely interested in helping students find what they want, whether it be an internship on Capitol Hill, job shadowing during the summer, a summer job with a law firm, or permanent placement with a company following graduation. Colgate alumni have great faith in the students at Colgate, and are always informing the staff at the Center with job opportunities and internships in their respective fields. Students in search of employment can network Colgate graduates listed in a database at the Center for job interviews, applications, or simple advice and guidance. The Center for Career Services regularly invites alumni to return to campus, and give seminars and lectures for students interested in their fields. It also encourages students to sign up for networking receptions where they meet Colgate graduates and exchange business information and personal knowledge.

Advice

- Get comfortable visiting the Center for Career Services—they sincerely want to help.
- Visit the Center early, even during freshman year. It never hurts to explore all your options.
- If you are unsure of what you want, talk to the staff, they will be able to help you figure out where you need to go.
- Utilize the mock interviews and resumé writing sessions! They are held often and are great tools.
- Do not be afraid to tell them what you want. The more specific you are, the easier they will be in locating something that fits you best.

Career Center Resources & Services

- Cover letters & other job search correspondence
- Résumé consultation
- Mock interview sessions
- Informational interviews
- Company research
- Graduate school guides
- Full-time positions
- Off-campus recruiting consortia
- Internship positions

Firms That Most Frequently Hire Graduates

Abercrombie & Fitch, American Express Financial Advisors, AmeriCorps, Bear Stearns, Boston Medical Center, Cadwalader, Wickersham & Taft LLP, Charles River Associates, Chubb Group of Insurance Companies, Citigroup, Cleary, Gottlieb, Steen & Hamilton, Colgate University, Commonwealth of Massachusetts, Cravath, Swaine & Moore LLP, Credit Suisse First Boston, Developers Diversified Realty Corporation, Deutsche Bank Securities, Inc., Economists Inc., Ernst & Younq LLP, ESPN, Goldman Sachs, Goodwin Proctor LLP, Harvard University Medical School, Hughes Hubbard & Reed, ICF Consulting, Johnson & Johnson, JPMorgan Chase, Lazard Freres, Leukemia & Lymphoma Society, Lockheed Martin, M & T Bank, MarketBridge, Massachusetts General Hospital, Massey Knakal Realty Services, Inc., McCann Erickson, Merrill Lynch, Morgan Stanley, National Institutes of Health, New England Center for Children, Paul, Weiss, Rifkind, Wharton & Garrison LLP, Peace Corps, PricewaterhouseCoopers LLP, Sidley Austin Brown & Wood, Smith Barney, St. Johnsbury Academy, State Street Corporation, TBWA/Chiat/Day, Teach For America, U. S. Department of Justice, UBS Warburg, Unilever Best Foods North America, Wachovia Securities, Weil Gotshal & Manges LLP, Williams & Connelly LLP, Young & Rubicam Advertising

Alumni

The Lowdown On...
Alumni

Web Site:
www.colgatealumni.org

E-Mail:
alumni@colgatealumni.org

Office:
Office of Alumni Affairs
Colgate University
13 Oak Drive
Hamilton, NY 13346
(315) 228-1000

Services Available:

Classifieds

The Alumni Office offers assistance in locating anything, from jobs to apartments, roommates, vacation properties, and miscellaneous items. Only members have access to the online database, and it is updated regularly with each ad.

Permanent E-Mail

Graduates may request another e-mail address when their original one, which they were given upon matriculation, expires.

→

→

(Services, continued)

Alumni Directory

The alumni directory, which can be accessed online, keeps track of all Colgate alums and is constantly being updated.

Cornell Club Membership

Upon graduating, Colgate alumni are given the opportunity to join the Cornell Club of New York. The club is affiliated with graduates from Cornell University, Brown University, Duke University, Georgetown University, the University of Notre Dame, Stanford University, and Tulane University. The graduates make up the largest portion, but family members and business associates are also welcome.

Williams Club Membership

Williams has the oldest existing Alumni Society, and in 1913, New York City Williams alumni founded the Williams Club of New York, and later extended its membership to other prestigious institutions, including Colgate. Members enjoy the benefits of fine gourmet dining, hotel rooms, and an elegant location to meet with friends, family, and associations for varying occasions. They may take advantage of the Madison Avenue location or any of its reciprocal clubs. The Club offers private banquet rooms, club programs and events, and fitness facilities.

Major Alumni Events

Homecoming – Every year alumni are invited to attend Colgate's Homecoming weekend. Many stay in area locations and visit campus. The University raises tents and conducts a tailgate before the football game, and special events, such as ice cream socials and meet and greets, are held annually.

Reunion – Reunion weekend is a four-day vacation usually held the first weekend in June. Alums return to the Chenango valley and enjoy the "spirit that is Colgate."

Alumni Publications

The Colgate Scene is published monthly, and informs Colgate alums of the latest alumni news. It can be accessed online through the Web site at *www.colgatealumni.org*.

Student Organizations

Academic

Colgate Pre-Med Student Association

Economics and Business Club

German Club

International Relations Council

Philosophy and Religion Club

Pre-Law Society

Psychology Club

SOAN Club (Sociology & Anthropology)

Spanish Club

Entertainment

Cecelie's Coffee House

Charred Goosebeak

Colgate Activities Board (CAB)

Student Committee On Providing Entertainment (SCOPE)

Take Two Film Committee

Spring Party Weekend Committee

Publications & Media

The Colgate Maroon-News (newspaper)

Colgate Buzzard

Colgate Portfolio

CUTV

Environmental Review

Prism (newspaper)

Salmagundi (yearbook)

WRCU-FM

Music, Drama, & Dance

Ballet Club

Colgate Chamber Players

Colgate Jazz Band

Colgate Thirteen (a cappella singers)

Colgate University Orchestra

Colgate's Groove

The Dischords (coed a cappella singers)

Kuumba (dance troupe)

Latin American Dancers

Legacy Dance Group

Raider Pep Band

Resolutions

Sojourners (gospel choir)

Student Musical Theater

Student Drama Society

Swing Club

Swinging 'Gates (a cappella singers)

University Chorus

University Theater

Urban Theater

We Funk

Political & Cultural

African American Student Alliance (AASA)
Asian Awareness Coalition
BROTHERS
Caribbean Student Association (CSA)
China Club
Colgate Greens
Colgate International Community (CIC)
Colgate Students for Change
College Democrats
College Republicans
Korean Students Association (KSA)
Filipine Student Association (FSA)
Latin American Student Organization (LASO)
Native American Student Association
Rainbow Alliance (Lesbian, Gay, Bisexual, Transgender)
South Asian Continental Club (SACC)
Sisters of the Round Table
Students for Environmental Awareness (SEA)
Students for Social Justice

The Best & Worst

The Ten BEST Things About Colgate

1. The happy medium between an attentive, small liberal arts college with the resources of a major university
2. Everybody stays on campus on the weekends, so during a late-night Slices run, you'll see about half the student body.
3. The renowned, highly-published, impressive, and overwhelmingly accessible staff
4. The beautiful campus buildings and grounds set in the rolling hills of the Chenango Valley
5. The well-balanced academics and parties; Colgate students work hard—and play harder
6. The tremendous amount of research opportunities and internships for undergraduates. Professors and career services can't seem to stop offering jobs, internships, and research opportunities.

7 Class dinners, field trips, and one-on-one attention from professors. We love Merill House, a full-service faculty dining hall often used to host class dinners.

8 The wide variety of student organizations and chances for leadership. Because the school is small, students can easily rise to leadership positions.

9 Graduation weekend—a torchlight parade of departing seniors, followed by dancing and drinking in the streets of downtown Hamilton.

10 The strong and supportive alumni base

The Ten WORST Things About Colgate

1. Course registration

2. The hit or miss quality of professors—sometimes the class is great, but the professor is horrible; sometimes the professor is great, but the class is horrible.

3. The bitterly cold winters

4. The huge variety in dormitories—'Gate House double versus Andrews suites

5. The housing lottery

6. The lack of variety in food options at the main dining halls and in town

7. The lack of places to party other than frats, dorms, and bars

8. The dying Greek presence

9. Having to climb up the hill after partying or parking your car

10. The lack of computers at the libraries during midterms and exam weeks

Visiting

The Lowdown On... Visiting

Hotel and Bed & Breakfast Information

Most of the available lodging facilities near Colgate are bed and breakfasts. All of these locations, along with a few others, can be found at *www.hamiltonny.com*, under lodging.

Automotive LLC Guest House

16 E. Pleasant St.

(315) 391-7933

(Automotive LLC, continued)

Distance from Campus: 2 minutes

Price Range: $85–$150

Bridle Creek B & B

5519 Hill Rd.

(315) 824-1962

Distance from Campus: 10 minutes

Price Range: All rooms $90

→

Charlotte Amalie Inn
4694 Park St.
(315) 684-3555
Distance from Campus: 10 minutes
Price Range: $150–$175

Colgate Inn
1 Payne St.
(315) 824-2300
www.colgateinn.com
Distance from Campus: 2 minutes
Price Range: $115–$275

Deer Meadows B & B
2846 West Hill Rd.
(315) 750-8964
Distance from Campus: 7 minutes
Price Range: All rooms $90

Hamilton Inn
2586 E. Lake Rd.
(315) 824-1245
Distance from Campus: 5 minutes
Price Range: $90–$170

Peaceful Pines B & B
6125 Briggs Rd.
(315) 824-2469
www.peacefulpines.com
Distance from Campus: 10 minutes
Price Range: $75–$125

Preston Hill B & B
1004 Preston Hill Rd.
(315) 691-5110
Distance from Campus: 5 minutes
Price Range: Cabin suite $200

White Eagle Conference Center
PO Box 679
(800) 295-9322
Distance from Campus: 5 minutes
Price Range: $89–$109

Ye Old Landmark Tavern
Route 20
(315) 893)-1810
Distance from Campus: 8 minutes
Price Range: $85–$130

Take a Campus Virtual Tour

www.colgate.edu; click on the link on the column on the right hand side of the screen.

To Schedule a group information session or interview:

Summer Hours: 8 a.m.–4:30 p.m., Monday through Friday.

Academic Year Hours: 8 a.m.–5 p.m., Monday through Friday. The office is open on select Saturdays.

Consult the schedule below, call (315) 228-7401, or e-mail at admission@mail.colgate.edu for more information.

The office is located in James B. Colgate Hall, where all campus tours begin. Information sessions are led by an admission officer and typically are held in the lobby of the Office of Admission. Sessions last about an hour and are given year-round. Information sessions and campus tours are held on a walk-in basis Monday–Friday. Call the Office of Admission if you plan to attend a Saturday session or tour. If you would like to meet with a coach during your time at Colgate, contact the Athletics Department prior to your arrival on campus.

Campus Tours

Tours last approximately 75 minutes. Tours are given by students, and therefore, are not available at all times.

Overnight Visits

The Student Host Program provides high school seniors and prospective transfer students an opportunity to experience everyday life at Colgate by staying overnight with a current student. Overnight visits during the week may include participating in classes and activities, eating in the dining hall, meeting with faculty, and speaking with current students. Hosts are available Sunday through Thursday, from mid-September to mid-November, and February to early March. Stays are limited to one night. Contact the Office of Admission at least two weeks in advance to arrange for a host.

Saturdays@Colgate are offered on Saturdays from mid-September to early December. Prospective students and their families can get an in-depth look at the academic and campus life at Colgate. Ideal for first-time visitors, Saturdays@Colgate offer an hour-long information session led by an admission officer, and the opportunity to hear from a faculty member and Colgate students. Immediately following the session, families are invited to join our student guides for a tour of the campus. Light refreshments will be available starting at 9:30 a.m., and the formal program begins at 10:00 a.m. A reservation is required for a Saturdays@Colgate program. Call the Office of Admission at (315) 228-7401.

Directions to Campus

Driving from the North

From Boston:

- Mass. Pike to NYS Thruway (connect I-87 North, I-90 West toward Buffalo)
- Take exit 25A and follow I-88 south to the first exit
- Pick up Route 20 west; at Madison, south on 12B

Driving from the East

From Philadelphia:

- Take Northeast Extension of PA Turnpike to I-81 at Scranton; north on I-81 to Binghamton
- Exit 6 for Route 12 north to Sherburne
- Bear left on 12B north to Hamilton

From North Central N.J.:

- Follow I-80 West. Exit to I-380 northwest toward Scranton, to I-81 north to Binghamton
- Exit 6 for Route 12 north to Sherburne, and 12B to Hamilton

From New York Metropolitan area:

- The Tappan Zee Bridge (NYS Thruway) to Route 17 west (Exit 16) to Deposit (Exit 84)
- At Deposit, right on Route 8 north to New Berlin, then Route 80 west to Sherburne.
- Right on Route 12, then bear left on Route 12B to Hamilton

Driving from the West

- Take the NYS Thruway east to Exit 33 (Vernon) to Route 365 west
- In Oneida, pick up Route 5 west and move to the left lanes, to catch left turn onto Route 46 south
- Follow 46 south, crossing Route 20, and onto Route 12B south into Hamilton

Words to Know

Academic Probation – A suspension imposed on a student if he or she fails to keep up with the school's minimum academic requirements. Those unable to improve their grades after receiving this warning can face dismissal.

Beer Pong/Beirut – A drinking game involving cups of beer arranged in a pyramid shape on each side of a table. The goal is to get a ping-pong ball into one of the opponent's cups by throwing the ball or hitting it with a paddle. If the ball lands in a cup, the opponent is required to drink the beer.

Bid – An invitation from a fraternity or sorority to 'pledge' (join) that specific house.

Blue-Light Phone – Brightly-colored phone posts with a blue light bulb on top. These phones exist for security purposes and are located at various outside locations around most campuses. In an emergency, a student can pick up one of these phones (free of charge) to connect with campus police or a security escort.

Campus Police – Police who are specifically assigned to a given institution. Campus police are typically not regular city officers; they are employed by the university in a full-time capacity.

Club Sports – A level of sports that falls somewhere between varsity and intramural. If a student is unable to commit to a varsity team but has a lot of passion for athletics, a club sport could be a better, less intense option. Even less demanding, intramural (IM) sports often involve no traveling and considerably less time.

Cocaine – An illegal drug. Also known as "coke" or "blow," cocaine often resembles a white crystalline or powdery substance. It is highly addictive and dangerous.

Common Application – An application with which students can apply to multiple schools.

Course Registration – The period of official class selection for the upcoming quarter or semester. Prior to registration, it is best to prepare several back-up courses in case a particular class becomes full. If a course is full, students can place themselves on the waitlist, although this still does not guarantee entry.

Division Athletics – Athletic classifications range from Division I to Division III. Division IA is the most competitive, while Division III is considered to be the least competitive.

Dorm – A dorm (or dormitory) is an on-campus housing facility. Dorms can provide a range of options from suite-style rooms to more communal options that include shared bathrooms. Most first-year students live in dorms. Some upperclassmen who wish to stay on campus also choose this option.

Early Action – An application option with which a student can apply to a school and receive an early acceptance response without a binding commitment. This system is becoming less and less available.

Early Decision – An application option that students should use only if they are certain they plan to attend the school in question. If a student applies using the early decision option and is admitted, he or she is required and bound to attend that university. Admission rates are usually higher among students who apply through early decision, as the student is clearly indicating that the school is his or her first choice.

Ecstasy – An illegal drug. Also known as "E" or "X," ecstasy looks like a pill and most resembles an aspirin. Considered a party drug, ecstasy is very dangerous and can be deadly.

Ethernet – An extremely fast Internet connection available in most university-owned residence halls. To use an Ethernet connection properly, a student will need a network card and cable for his or her computer.

Fake ID – A counterfeit identification card that contains false information. Most commonly, students get fake IDs with altered birthdates so that they appear to be older than 21 (and therefore of legal drinking age). Even though it is illegal, many college students have fake IDs in hopes of purchasing alcohol or getting into bars.

Frosh – Slang for "freshman" or "freshmen."

Hazing – Initiation rituals administered by some fraternities or sororities as part of the pledging process. Many universities have outlawed hazing due to its degrading and sometimes dangerous nature.

Intramurals (IMs) – A popular, and usually free, sport league in which students create teams and compete against one another. These sports vary in competitiveness and can include a range of activities—everything from billiards to water polo. IM sports are a great way to meet people with similar interests.

Keg – Officially called a half-barrel, a keg contains roughly 200 12-ounce servings of beer.

LSD – An illegal drug. Also known as acid, this hallucinogenic drug most commonly resembles a tab of paper.

Marijuana – An illegal drug. Also known as weed or pot; along with alcohol, marijuana is one of the most commonly-found drugs on campuses across the country.

Major –The focal point of a student's college studies; a specific topic that is studied for a degree. Examples of majors include physics, English, history, computer science, economics, business, and music. Many students decide on a specific major before arriving on campus, while others are simply "undecided" until declaring a major. Those who are extremely interested in two areas can also choose to double major.

Meal Block – The equivalent of one meal. Students on a meal plan usually receive a fixed number of meals per week. Each meal, or "block," can be redeemed at the school's dining facilities in place of cash. Often, a student's weekly allotment of meal blocks will be forfeited if not used.

Minor – An additional focal point in a student's education. Often serving as a complement or addition to a student's main area of focus, a minor has fewer requirements and prerequisites to fulfill than a major. Minors are not required for graduation from most schools; however some students who want to explore many different interests choose to pursue both a major and a minor.

Mushrooms – An illegal drug. Also known as "'shrooms," this drug resembles regular mushrooms but is extremely hallucinogenic.

Off-Campus Housing – Housing from a particular landlord or rental group that is not affiliated with the university. Depending on the college, off-campus housing can range from extremely popular to non-existent. Students who choose to live off campus are typically given more freedom, but they also have to deal with possible subletting scenarios, furniture, bills, and other issues. In addition to these factors, rental prices and distance often affect a student's decision to move off campus.

Office Hours – Time that teachers set aside for students who have questions about coursework. Office hours are a good forum for students to go over any problems and to show interest in the subject material.

Pledging – The early phase of joining a fraternity or sorority, pledging takes place after a student has gone through rush and received a bid. Pledging usually lasts between one and two semesters. Once the pledging period is complete and a particular student has done everything that is required to become a member, that student is considered a brother or sister. If a fraternity or a sorority would decide to "haze" a group of students, this initiation would take place during the pledging period.

Private Institution – A school that does not use tax revenue to subsidize education costs. Private schools typically cost more than public schools and are usually smaller.

Prof – Slang for "professor."

Public Institution – A school that uses tax revenue to subsidize education costs. Public schools are often a good value for in-state residents and tend to be larger than most private colleges.

Quarter System (or Trimester System) – A type of academic calendar system. In this setup, students take classes for three academic periods. The first quarter usually starts in late September or early October and concludes right before Christmas. The second quarter usually starts around early to mid–January and finishes up around March or April. The last academic quarter, or "third quarter," usually starts in late March or early April and finishes up in late May or Mid-June. The fourth quarter is summer. The major difference between the quarter system and semester system is that students take more, less comprehensive courses under the quarter calendar.

RA (Resident Assistant) – A student leader who is assigned to a particular floor in a dormitory in order to help to the other students who live there. An RA's duties include ensuring student safety and providing assistance wherever possible.

Recitation – An extension of a specific course; a review session. Some classes, particularly large lectures, are supplemented with mandatory recitation sessions that provide a relatively personal class setting.

Rolling Admissions – A form of admissions. Most commonly found at public institutions, schools with this type of policy continue to accept students throughout the year until their class sizes are met. For example, some schools begin accepting students as early as December and will continue to do so until April or May.

Room and Board – This figure is typically the combined cost of a university-owned room and a meal plan.

Room Draw/Housing Lottery – A common way to pick on-campus room assignments for the following year. If a student decides to remain in university-owned housing, he or she is assigned a unique number that, along with seniority, is used to determine his or her housing for the next year.

Rush – The period in which students can meet the brothers and sisters of a particular chapter and find out if a given fraternity or sorority is right for them. Rushing a fraternity or a sorority is not a requirement at any school. The goal of rush is to give students who are serious about pledging a feel for what to expect.

Semester System – The most common type of academic calendar system at college campuses. This setup typically includes two semesters in a given school year. The fall semester starts around the end of August or early September and concludes before winter vacation. The spring semester usually starts in mid-January and ends in late April or May.

Student Center/Rec Center/Student Union – A common area on campus that often contains study areas, recreation facilities, and eateries. This building is often a good place to meet up with fellow students; depending on the school, the student center can have a huge role or a non-existent role in campus life.

Student ID – A university-issued photo ID that serves as a student's key to school-related functions. Some schools require students to show these cards in order to get into dorms, libraries, cafeterias, and other facilities. In addition to storing meal plan information, in some cases, a student ID can actually work as a debit card and allow students to purchase things from bookstores or local shops.

Suite – A type of dorm room. Unlike dorms that feature communal bathrooms shared by the entire floor, suites offer bathrooms shared only among the suite. Suite-style dorm rooms can house anywhere from two to ten students.

TA (Teacher's Assistant) – An undergraduate or grad student who helps in some manner with a specific course. In some cases, a TA will teach a class, assist a professor, grade assignments, or conduct office hours.

Undergraduate – A student in the process of studying for his or her bachelor's degree.

ABOUT THE AUTHORS

During my numerous college tours, I visited Colgate on a whim because a friend of mine was about to attend and we were in the area. I automatically fell in love with it during that first visit. The grounds and facilities were beautiful, and my tour guide obviously loved his school. I was accepted to other prestigious institutions in addition to Colgate, making my decision a bit more difficult. Then I stayed overnight during the spring of my senior year, and the love was rekindled. I knew Colgate was the right choice when I saw how much happier and enthusiastic the students at Colgate were than at any other institution I had visited, and they were not all cheerleaders. That was when I met Elisa, a spunky and energetic girl I really hoped would make the same decision as me.

Contrasting Elisa, I am pursuing a dual concentration in sociology and anthropology, with a minor concentration in writing in the social sciences. I hope to graduate and pursue graduate education in law school or journalism school. I have maintained status on the Dean's List and received the Dean's award for the past three semesters at Colgate, so hopefully those awards will help my acceptance.

As for me, Elisa, when I'm not hanging out with Des, I'm either working at the Writing Center or Colgate's PR office, writing my weekly relationship-commentary column for the school paper, spinning punk rock tunes on 'RCU, or heading up the Colgate Activities Board Special Events committee. Oh yeah, I also find time to go to class, where I'm working toward an art and art history concentration and an interdisciplinary writing minor. Here I am, loving every minute of college life, and hoping that my input with the College Prowler guide to Colgate will help others mail the right envelope, too.

Desirée Abeleda
desireeabeleda@collegeprowler.com

Elisa Benson
elisabenson@collegeprowler.com

New England Colleges

Looking for peace in the Northeast?

Pick up this regional guide to New England!

New England Colleges
7¼" X 10", 1015 Pages Paperback
$29.95 Retail
1-59658-504-8

New England is the birthplace of many prestigious universities, and with so many to choose from, picking the right school can be a tough decision. With inside information on over 34 competive Northeastern schools, *New England Colleges* provides the same high-quality information prospective students expect from College Prowler in one all-inclusive, easy-to-use reference.

Untangling the Ivy League

The ultimate book for everything Ivy!

Untangling the Ivy League
7¼" X 10", 567 Pages Paperback
$24.95 Retail
1-59658-500-5

Ivy League students, alumni, admissions officers, and other top insiders get together to tell it like it is. *Untangling the Ivy League* covers every aspect—from admissions and athletics to secret societies and urban legends—of the nation's eight oldest, wealthiest, and most competitive colleges and universities.

Need More Help?

Do you have more questions about this school? Can't find a certain statistic? College Prowler is here to help. We are the best source of college information out there. We have a network of thousands of students who can get the latest information on any school to you ASAP. E-mail us at info@collegeprowler.com with your college-related questions.

E-Mail Us Your College-Related Questions!

Check out ***www.collegeprowler.com*** for more details.
1-800-290-2682

Write For Us!

Get published! Voice your opinion.

Writing a College Prowler guidebook is both fun and rewarding; our open-ended format allows your own creativity free reign. Our writers have been featured in national newspapers and have seen their names in bookstores across the country. Now is your chance to break into the publishing industry with one of the country's fastest-growing publishers!

Apply now at ***www.collegeprowler.com***

Contact editor@collegeprowler.com or
call 1-800-290-2682 for more details.

Pros and Cons

Still can't figure out if this is the right school for you? You've already read through this in-depth guide; why not list the pros and cons? It will really help with narrowing down your decision and determining whether or not this school is right for you.

Pros	Cons
....	....
....	....
....	....
....	....
....	....
....	....
....	....
....	....
....	....
....	....
....	....
....	....
....	....

Pros and Cons

Still can't figure out if this is the right school for you? You've already read through this in-depth guide; why not list the pros and cons? It will really help with narrowing down your decision and determining whether or not this school is right for you.

Pros	Cons
....	....
....	....
....	....
....	....
....	....
....	....
....	....
....	....
....	....
....	....
....	....
....	....
....	....

Notes

Notes

Notes

Notes

Notes

Notes

Notes

Notes

Notes

Notes

Notes

Notes

Notes

COLLEGE PROWLER®

Notes

Notes

Notes

College Prowler®

Notes

Notes

Notes

College
Prowler